To my parents, whose love and values have shaped who I am.
To the timeless teachings of Swami Vivekananda, which continue to illuminate the path for countless souls.
And to every seeker on the journey of self-discovery, may you find the light within.

ZERO TO LAUNCH

BUILDING YOUR BUSINESS FROM SCRATCH

SWAPNIL KHAMKAR

Contents

Contents

Contents

Foreword

Entrepreneurship is more than just building a business—it's about crafting a vision, embracing risks, and transforming ideas into impactful realities. In today's fast-paced world, where opportunities and challenges evolve rapidly, the ability to navigate uncertainty with confidence is what sets great entrepreneurs apart.

"Zero to Launch: Building Your Business from Scratch" is not just another book on starting a business. It is a powerful blueprint for aspiring entrepreneurs, equipping them with the mindset, strategies, and practical insights needed to build, grow, and sustain a successful venture.

The beauty of this book lies in its simplicity and depth. It does not merely provide theoretical knowledge but offers a roadmap that is both inspiring and actionable. Whether you are just beginning your entrepreneurial journey or looking to refine your approach, this book will serve as a trusted companion—guiding you through the complexities of the startup world with clarity and wisdom.

The entrepreneurial journey is not a solitary one. It thrives on learning, adaptation, and the courage to take bold steps. This book encapsulates these elements beautifully, making it an essential read for anyone with the ambition to create, innovate, and make a meaningful impact.

I wholeheartedly recommend *Zero to Launch* to every dreamer, doer, and disruptor ready to turn their vision into reality. May this book ignite your entrepreneurial spirit and lead you to incredible success.

— *Sanjay Khamkar*

Preface

The journey from an idea to a thriving business is one filled with excitement, challenges, and countless learning experiences. Every successful entrepreneur begins at the same place—zero. The difference lies in how they take that first step and the choices they make along the way.

This book, *Zero to Launch: Building Your Business from Scratch*, was born out of a deep desire to simplify the entrepreneurial process and provide a structured, practical guide for those ready to embark on this path. Through years of research, experience, and observations of successful ventures, I have compiled key lessons, actionable strategies, and real-world insights that will help you navigate the complexities of starting and scaling a business.

Entrepreneurship is not reserved for the privileged few—it is for anyone with a vision and the determination to bring it to life. Whether you are a student with an idea, a professional looking to transition into business, or an entrepreneur aiming to refine your approach, this book is designed to be your step-by-step guide.

My hope is that *Zero to Launch* not only equips you with knowledge but also instils in you the confidence to take action. The world needs more creators, innovators, and change-makers—perhaps, you are one of them.

So, let's begin. Your journey from zero to launch starts now.

— *Swapnil Khamkar*

Acknowledgements

This book would not have been possible without the love, guidance, and support of so many incredible individuals who have been a part of my journey.

First and foremost, I express my deepest gratitude to my parents, Sanjay Khamkar and Pratibha Khamkar, for their unconditional love and for instilling in me the values that guide my life. To my beloved wife, Yashasvi Khamkar, thank you for being my partner in every sense; your unwavering support means the world to me.

To Pushpak Khamkar and Vrushali Khamkar, your encouragement has been a pillar of strength. I also honor the blessings of my grandparents, Harishchandra Khamkar and Taramati Khamkar, whose love and wisdom have shaped me profoundly.

I extend heartfelt thanks to my mentors, Prof. Dr. Vasant Desale sir and Prof. Ganpat Shelke sir, whose guidance and insights have inspired me to achieve more than I thought possible.

I owe a deep sense of gratitude to the timeless teachings of Swami Vivekananda, whose wisdom and vision continue to inspire and guide me every single day. His philosophy has profoundly influenced my personal journey and the vision of this book.

Lastly, to my readers: thank you for choosing this book and for being a part of this journey. Your willingness to explore new perspectives and embark on a path of transformation gives meaning to this work.

With profound gratitude,
Swapnil Khamkar

CHAPTER I

India's Economic Landscape: A Journey to New Heights

India's Economic Momentum and the Power of Its Youth

India stands at a defining moment in its economic journey. With a population of over 1.4 billion and a rich cultural heritage, the country has emerged as a global powerhouse, fueled by resilience and ambition. In 2023, India's economy hit a significant milestone, with its GDP reaching $3.89 trillion in FY 2024 and a growth rate of 7.0%, making it the fastest-growing major economy in the world.

The Youth Factor: Strength and Challenge

One of India's greatest strengths is its youthful population—over 808 million people under the age of 35. This generation has the potential to drive unprecedented progress, but unlocking that potential requires overcoming critical challenges.

Key Challenges Facing India's Youth

1. Unemployment Crisis
India's youth unemployment rate rose to 8% in 2024, with rural unemployment jumping from 5.8% to 7.8%. Job creation must keep pace with the growing workforce to

prevent talent from going untapped.

2. Mental Health Concerns

Nearly 15% of Indians face mental health struggles, including depression and anxiety. A lack of awareness and support systems only deepens the crisis, making mental health intervention a necessity.

3. Mismatched Aspirations and Reality

Many young Indians find themselves in careers that don't align with their interests or skills, leading to dissatisfaction and disengagement. The gap between educational training and job market demands remains a major issue.

4. Social and Cultural Barriers

Issues like substance abuse, gender discrimination, and communal tensions create an unstable environment, limiting opportunities for many.

5. Education Gaps

Outdated curricula, high tuition fees, and a disconnect between academic training and industry needs leave many graduates unprepared for real-world challenges.

6. Rising Competition and Pressure

With intense competition in academics and careers, societal expectations push many young individuals toward stress, burnout, and mental fatigue.

7. Inflation and Cost of Living

Rising prices make basic necessities increasingly unaffordable, particularly for lower-income groups, demanding urgent economic policies to ease the financial burden.

The Road Ahead

India's youth are not just its future—they are its present. By investing in education reform, mental health awareness, skill development, and job creation, the country can turn these challenges into opportunities. With the right policies and collective effort, India has the potential to not only empower its young population but also set a global example of how economic progress and youthful ambition can shape a thriving nation.

CHAPTER II

Vision for India's Future

India's Path to a Transformative Future

India stands on the brink of a new era, with the potential to turn its demographic advantage into unprecedented growth and development. With the right focus and commitment, the nation can pave the way for a brighter, more inclusive future. To achieve this, India must prioritize key areas that will drive economic progress, social equity, and sustainability.

Fostering Entrepreneurship and Innovation

A thriving economy is built on innovation and entrepreneurial spirit. India must nurture an environment that encourages bold ideas, risk-taking, and enterprise development. Access to funding, mentorship, and modern infrastructure will empower entrepreneurs to create solutions for local and global challenges while driving large-scale job creation.

Investing in Human Capital

India's true strength lies in its people. Quality education, accessible healthcare, and skill development programs tailored to a dynamic economy will ensure a workforce that is competent, confident, and future-ready. A nation that invests in its human capital secures long-term growth and prosperity.

Inclusive and Equitable Growth

Progress is meaningful only when it reaches every segment of society. Bridging social and economic disparities, addressing regional imbalances, and championing gender equality will create a more inclusive India. When opportunities are evenly distributed, the collective strength of the nation multiplies.

Sustainability and Environmental Responsibility

Economic growth must go hand in hand with environmental sustainability. Embracing green technologies, investing in renewable energy, and adopting eco-friendly practices will safeguard India's natural resources while positioning the country as a global leader in climate action.

Global Influence and Leadership

India's rich cultural heritage, economic potential, and diplomatic influence give it a unique opportunity to shape global affairs. By leveraging its economic strength and soft power, India can play a crucial role in addressing pressing global challenges and reinforcing its leadership on the world stage.

India's Thriving Startup Ecosystem

India's startup ecosystem is a testament to the country's entrepreneurial spirit and innovative mindset. As one of the world's fastest-growing startup hubs, it continues to evolve, setting new benchmarks in the global business landscape.

A Rapidly Expanding Startup Culture

India is home to over 75,000 startups, making it one of the largest and most dynamic startup ecosystems in the world. With a consistent annual growth rate of 18-22%, the sector showcases resilience, adaptability, and an unyielding drive for innovation.

Attracting Global Investments

Investor confidence remains high, with annual startup funding crossing $15 billion. Both domestic and international investors recognize the potential of India's entrepreneurial landscape, driving substantial capital inflows into emerging businesses.

Expanding the Unicorn Club

India continues to produce unicorns—startups valued at over $1 billion—at an impressive pace. These success stories span industries like fintech, e-commerce, healthtech, and SaaS, reinforcing the country's reputation as a hub for high-growth ventures.

Beyond Metropolitan Hubs

While Bengaluru, Mumbai, and Delhi have traditionally dominated the startup scene, cities like Hyderabad, Chennai, and Pune are now thriving innovation centers. Even tier-2 and tier-3 cities are making significant contributions, ensuring entrepreneurship is not limited to urban elites but accessible to a wider population.

Shifting Industry Trends

While fintech and e-commerce remain dominant, new sectors such as healthtech, SaaS, and renewable energy are gaining traction. Startups addressing global priorities like climate change and sustainability are emerging as key players, aligning India with international economic trends.

A Driving Force for Employment

Startups are not just innovation hubs; they are vital employment generators. Directly employing millions of people and supporting many more through allied industries, startups provide essential opportunities for India's vast young workforce.

Resilience and Future Outlook

India's startup ecosystem has repeatedly proven its resilience, navigating economic shifts and technological disruptions with agility. As regulatory support improves and investment continues to flow, the momentum is set to accelerate. With its unmatched talent, creativity, and ambition, India's startup ecosystem is poised to redefine the global business landscape.

CHAPTER III

Startup Scenario in India

India's Startup Ecosystem: A Thriving Hub of Innovation

India's startup landscape is a dynamic force of innovation, resilience, and economic transformation. With its ability to disrupt industries and tackle global challenges, the country's entrepreneurial ecosystem is rapidly gaining worldwide recognition.

The Rise of Unicorns

India has emerged as a powerhouse for unicorns—startups valued at over $1 billion—across diverse sectors such as e-commerce, fintech, healthtech, and edtech. These companies are not only reshaping traditional industries but also positioning India as a global leader in innovation.

Beyond their financial success, unicorns serve as inspiration for aspiring entrepreneurs, proving that bold ideas and perseverance can lead to groundbreaking achievements on the global stage.

Government Support and Policy Initiatives

The Indian government has played a crucial role in fostering entrepreneurship through initiatives like Startup India, Standup India, and the Atal Innovation Mission. These programs provide essential support, including funding, mentorship, and infrastructure, helping startups overcome initial hurdles and scale their businesses.

State governments have also stepped in with region-specific policies to promote local entrepreneurship, ensuring that the benefits of innovation extend beyond metropolitan hubs.

The Role of Venture Capital and Investments

Investment has been a key driver of India's startup boom. Venture capitalists, angel investors, and crowdfunding platforms have injected substantial capital into promising ventures, allowing startups to scale rapidly and explore new markets.

India's growing consumer base and technological advancements continue to attract both domestic and international investors, reinforcing confidence in the ecosystem's long-term potential.

Innovation as the Driving Force

Indian startups are at the forefront of cutting-edge technologies like artificial intelligence (AI), machine learning (ML), blockchain, and augmented reality (AR). What sets them apart is their ability to adapt innovation to local challenges, including healthcare accessibility, financial inclusion, and digital education.

This commitment to technological advancement ensures that Indian startups remain globally competitive while also addressing grassroots issues that impact millions.

Challenges and Opportunities

Despite its success, the Indian startup ecosystem faces hurdles such as regulatory complexities, talent shortages, and market volatility. However, these challenges present opportunities for disruption in e-commerce, healthcare, education, and renewable energy—sectors poised for exponential growth.

By navigating these challenges with resilience and adaptability, Indian startups can unlock their full potential and contribute significantly to the country's economic and social progress.

A Future Shaped by Innovation

India's startup ecosystem is more than a business revolution—it's a movement that's reshaping the future. With strong policy support, increasing investments, and a growing pool of talented entrepreneurs, India is well on its way to becoming a global innovation powerhouse.

As startups continue to push boundaries, solve critical problems, and drive economic transformation, the future holds limitless possibilities. India's entrepreneurial journey is not just about building businesses—it's about creating a world of opportunity, progress, and lasting impact.

CHAPTER IV

Startups: From Idea to Reality

Startups are born at the crossroads of creativity, ambition, and innovation. They are more than just businesses in their early stages—they are bold ideas brought to life. What begins as a simple vision can evolve into a transformative force, reshaping industries and unlocking new opportunities. However, the journey from concept to success is filled with challenges, learning experiences, and the need for relentless persistence.

What Makes a Startup Unique?

Unlike traditional businesses, startups are driven by the desire to introduce something new to the market—an innovative product, service, or solution that fills a gap. Entrepreneurs behind these ventures do more than just run operations; they craft business strategies, secure funding, and refine their offerings to meet real-world demands. Protecting intellectual property, whether through trademarks, patents, or copyrights, is essential in ensuring that these ideas remain distinct and competitive.

Laying the Foundation for a Startup

Every successful startup begins with thorough preparation. Market research is the first crucial step—understanding potential customers, analyzing competitors, and identifying industry trends. A compelling brand identity follows, one that resonates with the vision and establishes a strong online presence. Entrepreneurs also need to protect their intellectual property early on to safeguard their unique concepts.

Beyond groundwork, choosing the right business model is essential. Some startups aim to address social or environmental issues, while others focus on rapid scalability. Some ventures are deeply personal, aligning with lifestyle choices rather than aggressive market expansion. Identifying the right path determines the direction a startup will take.

A business plan serves as a roadmap, outlining how the startup will generate revenue, what makes it unique, and how financial sustainability will be achieved. Securing funding then becomes the next big step. While some entrepreneurs rely on personal savings or support from family and friends, others seek bank loans, venture capital, angel investors, or crowdfunding to scale their operations.

The Role of Guidance and Mentorship

No entrepreneur builds a successful venture alone. Seeking mentorship and networking within the industry can accelerate growth. Programs like business incubators and accelerators provide resources, mentorship, and sometimes even financial backing. Experienced professionals in legal, marketing, and financial domains can offer crucial insights that prevent costly mistakes.

As the startup moves closer to launch, refining the product or service becomes a priority. A strong marketing strategy helps create early traction, while a test launch provides valuable feedback. Adaptability is key—what works on paper may need adjustments in the real market.

Bringing a Startup to Life

The official launch marks the beginning of the entrepreneurial journey, but it is far from the end. Execution is everything. Entrepreneurs must monitor performance, analyze results, and pivot when necessary. The ability to adapt and evolve determines long-term success.

Every startup follows a structured lifecycle. It begins with a problem that sparks an idea, followed by research and validation. Legal and operational frameworks are put in place before securing funding. The final step is market entry—launching, analyzing feedback, and scaling up.

The Entrepreneurial Road Ahead

Success in the startup world is not just about reaching milestones—it is about the journey of innovation, resilience, and continuous growth. Every major company today, from tech giants to industry disruptors, once started as just an idea in someone's mind. With a clear vision, strategic execution, and the right support, any startup has the potential to shape the future.

CHAPTER V

Entrepreneurship: An Introduction

The Entrepreneurial Mindset: Vision, Innovation, and Growth

An entrepreneur is more than just a business owner; they are visionaries who take risks, organize resources, and build ventures that create lasting impact. They bring ideas to life, develop enterprises around them, and contribute to society through their independent efforts. While small business owners and entrepreneurs share similarities, their ambitions, approaches, and outlooks set them apart.

Entrepreneurs operate with a vision for rapid growth, aiming to disrupt industries or create entirely new markets. Their focus goes beyond steady expansion—they seek to revolutionize the way businesses function and introduce transformative solutions. Small business owners, in contrast, often prioritize stability, aiming for gradual growth by expanding their customer base or diversifying their services over time.

A key distinction lies in their commitment to change. Small business owners make cautious adjustments, ensuring their operations remain steady. Entrepreneurs, however, thrive on innovation, constantly searching for opportunities to challenge the status quo. They introduce new products, services, and business models that address unmet needs and transform industries.

Resourcefulness is another defining trait. While small business owners often rely on traditional funding sources like savings or bank loans, entrepreneurs explore a wide range of options, including venture capital, angel investors, and crowdfunding. They take bold steps to secure the resources necessary for scaling their ideas into large enterprises. Their ultimate goal is to achieve extraordinary results, pushing beyond conventional boundaries and striving for breakthroughs that redefine markets.

The Essence of Entrepreneurship

At its core, entrepreneurship is about recognizing opportunities and pursuing them, even in the face of limited resources. It requires a combination of vision, action, and an unyielding drive to create meaningful change.

Successful entrepreneurs make crucial decisions under uncertainty, balancing risks and opportunities with confidence. They embrace challenges, turning setbacks into lessons and failures into stepping stones for growth. Risk management becomes second nature, as they evaluate potential threats and devise strategies to ensure long-term sustainability.

Beyond just starting a business, entrepreneurship is about building and leading organizations. Entrepreneurs assemble the right teams, establish efficient operations, and ensure that their ventures are positioned for long-term success. Innovation lies at the heart of their journey—introducing ideas, products, or solutions that solve pressing problems and create value.

From Idea to Reality

Entrepreneurs begin by identifying opportunities, using their creativity to spot gaps in the market. Once an idea takes shape, they conduct research and analysis to assess its feasibility and potential impact. They mobilize resources—capital, talent, and infrastructure—to transform their vision into a tangible enterprise.

Establishing a business involves more than just securing funding or launching a product. Entrepreneurs must navigate legal requirements, build brand identity, and set up operational frameworks that sustain growth. As their ventures take off, they take on the role of leaders, overseeing every aspect of the business—from financial planning to strategic expansion—ensuring profitability and long-term sustainability.

Entrepreneurship is not just about making money or starting a company; it's about embracing a mindset of innovation, resilience, and forward-thinking. Entrepreneurs are catalysts of progress, shaping the future with their bold ideas and determination. Their ability to adapt, take calculated risks, and envision possibilities where others see obstacles sets them apart as true architects of change.

CHAPTER VI

Taking the Leap into Entrepreneurship

The Entrepreneurial Decision: Is Starting a Business Right for You?

Starting a business is an exciting yet demanding journey. It begins with an idea, but turning that idea into reality requires time, effort, and careful consideration. Before diving in, it's important to take a step back and evaluate what's driving your entrepreneurial aspirations. Are you motivated by a passion for your work, the desire to create an impact, or the financial freedom that comes with running your own business? Understanding your true motivations will provide clarity and help you stay committed when challenges arise.

Building a business is a long-term commitment that involves wearing multiple hats, working longer hours, and taking on greater responsibilities. While the rewards—financial independence, personal fulfillment, and the opportunity to leave a lasting legacy—can be significant, the risks are just as real. Before making the leap, it's essential to weigh the benefits and challenges of entrepreneurship against the stability of traditional employment.

Employment vs. Entrepreneurship: Weighing Your Options

A traditional job offers financial security, a structured work environment, and benefits such as health insurance and paid leave. Many companies also invest in employee growth through training programs and career development opportunities. Working within an organization fosters a sense of stability, collaboration, and shared purpose. However, it also comes with limitations. Salary structures may cap earning potential, career progression can be slow, and rigid work hours can limit flexibility. Office politics, bureaucracy, and long commutes can add to the frustrations of being an employee.

On the other hand, running your own business opens up the potential for higher earnings, creative freedom, and greater control over your time. As an entrepreneur, your success is directly tied to your effort, vision, and decision-making. The satisfaction of building something from the ground up and seeing it thrive can be immensely fulfilling. However, it also means embracing uncertainty—there are no guaranteed paychecks, no employer-provided benefits, and no fixed work hours. The responsibility for every decision, success, and failure falls on your shoulders, making it crucial to develop resilience and adaptability.

For those hesitant to leave the security of a steady job, starting a business as a side venture can be a smart way to transition. It allows you to test your idea, build a customer base, and gain confidence while maintaining financial stability. Over time, as your business grows, you can assess whether to make the full shift to entrepreneurship.

Assessing Yourself: Are You Ready for Entrepreneurship?

Success in business is not just about having a great idea—it's about execution, adaptability, and self-awareness. Before stepping into the entrepreneurial world, take a moment to reflect on your strengths, weaknesses, and readiness for the challenges ahead.

What Makes You the Right Person for This Business?

Entrepreneurship requires a blend of vision and practicality. Ask yourself: Do you have the knowledge and skills necessary to bring your idea to life? Are you willing to acquire new skills or seek help in areas where you lack expertise? Not every entrepreneur starts fully prepared, but the ability to learn, adapt, and persist is what separates successful business owners from those who struggle.

Are You Equipped for the Challenges Ahead?

Consider the professional experience, talents, and skills you bring to the table. If you have expertise in leadership, budgeting, marketing, or negotiation, these abilities will be valuable as you build your business. On the other hand, acknowledging your weaknesses is just as important. If you lack experience in financial management, digital marketing, or business operations, it may be necessary to seek guidance, take courses, or partner with someone who complements your skills.

Is This the Right Time?

Timing plays a critical role in entrepreneurial success. Before making a decision, conduct thorough market research. Is there demand for your product or service? Who are your competitors, and how can you differentiate yourself? Seek insights from experienced entrepreneurs, and be realistic about the time, money, and effort required to build a successful business.

If you're currently employed, consider whether starting part-time is a viable option. Testing your business idea while maintaining a steady income can reduce financial risk and allow you to make informed decisions about scaling up.

Aligning Your Strengths and Interests with Your Business Idea

The most successful businesses are often built on a foundation of passion and expertise. Think about what excites you—your hobbies, interests, and past experiences. Do they align with your business idea? Your enthusiasm and knowledge in a particular field can give you a competitive edge and make the journey more rewarding.

Reflect on what drives you:

- Do you enjoy problem-solving, creating new things, or working with people?
- Are there skills or knowledge from your past experiences that could contribute to your business success?

- Is there a cause or industry you feel deeply passionate about?

Entrepreneurship is not just about financial gain; it's about creating something meaningful that aligns with your strengths, values, and aspirations.

Taking the Leap with Confidence

Starting a business is a major life decision, and preparation is key. By honestly assessing your skills, motivations, and readiness, you can set yourself up for a successful entrepreneurial journey. Aligning your business with your strengths and passions will not only increase your chances of success but also make the process more fulfilling.

There will always be risks and uncertainties, but with the right mindset, strategic planning, and willingness to learn, you can navigate the challenges and build a business that thrives. Whether you choose to start now or take more time to prepare, the most important step is believing in your vision and taking action.

CHAPTER VII

Developing Your Business Idea

From Idea to Business: Turning Inspiration into Opportunity

Every successful business begins with a spark of inspiration—an idea designed to solve a problem or improve an existing product or service. While the excitement of brainstorming new possibilities is invigorating, a great idea alone isn't enough. The journey from concept to reality requires careful evaluation to ensure the idea is not just exciting but also viable and positioned for long-term success.

Finding the Right Business Idea

The foundation of a strong business lies in identifying a genuine need in the market. Often, the best ideas emerge from noticing gaps—areas where existing products or services fall short or where innovation is lacking. A strong business concept taps into these unmet needs, offering something unique and valuable. Instead of competing in overcrowded markets, focusing on niche opportunities can provide a more loyal and engaged customer base.

Validating the Idea Through Market Research

Before investing time and resources, it's crucial to understand the landscape in which the business will operate. Staying informed about industry trends through online media, trade publications, and business forums can reveal emerging opportunities. However, research shouldn't be limited to passive observation—engaging directly with potential customers through surveys, interviews, and social media interactions provides deeper insights into their needs and expectations.

Competitive analysis is another essential step. Studying similar businesses and their successes—or shortcomings—can help refine a business idea, ensuring it stands out rather than blends in. Observing industry leaders and their strategies offers valuable lessons on market positioning and potential growth trajectories.

Assessing Feasibility and Market Potential

Even the most innovative ideas must be tested for practicality. Evaluating factors such as financial viability, resource availability, and potential risks can determine whether an idea has real potential or is merely an exciting concept. Business conditions change, and unforeseen challenges may arise, so conducting a strengths, weaknesses, opportunities, and threats (SWOT) analysis helps entrepreneurs develop strategies to navigate obstacles and maximize advantages.

A strong business idea isn't necessarily one that is completely risk-free—it's one with a clear strategy for overcoming challenges while leveraging strengths. If an idea meets key criteria—offering value, addressing a real need, and having growth potential—it is worth pursuing further.

The Characteristics of a Strong Business Idea

While no idea is perfect, successful businesses are built on concepts that meet essential criteria. A well-positioned business idea:

- Addresses a Market Gap – It provides a solution where demand exists but supply is insufficient.
- Innovates or Improves – It enhances existing products or services or offers a completely new approach.
- Challenges the Status Quo – It introduces a fresh way of solving problems or streamlining processes.
- Stands Out from the Competition – It has a clear differentiator that gives it an edge in the market.
- Meets Customer Expectations – It aligns with what consumers want and need, ensuring satisfaction and loyalty.
- Provides Real Value – It delivers benefits that justify the price, making it an attractive choice for consumers.
- Plays to Your Strengths – It leverages the entrepreneur's skills, experience, or industry knowledge.
- Operates in a Growing Market – It aligns with an expanding industry that offers long-term opportunities.
- Has the Potential to Scale – It can be expanded to reach more customers without excessive cost increases.

If a business idea checks most of these boxes, it has a strong foundation for success. However, proper execution and continuous adaptation are just as crucial as the idea itself.

Where Business Ideas Come From

Opportunities for business innovation can arise from multiple sources. Many entrepreneurs find inspiration by paying close attention to the world around them—identifying inefficiencies, listening to consumer demands, or spotting trends before they become mainstream.

- Existing Products or Services: Observing patterns of demand can reveal gaps where current offerings fall short, presenting clear entrepreneurial opportunities. Businesses that improve or expand upon existing solutions often gain traction quickly.
- Customer Insights: Direct interaction with consumers can uncover unmet needs. A business responding to customer frustrations or requests has a built-in demand from the start.
- Distribution and Supply Chain Innovation: Inefficiencies in logistics, retail, or production processes can be turned into business opportunities, making systems more effective and profitable.
- Government Initiatives and Investments: Public sector projects, grants, and infrastructure developments create business opportunities for contractors, suppliers, and service providers. Understanding government priorities can help entrepreneurs align their offerings with current needs.
- Research and Development: Companies that invest in continuous improvement and technological advancements can stay ahead of the curve. Whether enhancing existing products or creating new solutions, R&D-driven businesses often lead in their industries.

Entrepreneurship thrives on curiosity, creativity, and the ability to recognize opportunities where others see obstacles. The most successful businesses are built by those who stay informed, adapt quickly, and take decisive action.

Turning Insight into Action

A business idea alone holds no value unless it is brought to life through strategic planning and execution. While inspiration is the first step, what separates successful entrepreneurs from dreamers is their ability to validate, refine, and act on their ideas. With thorough research, a strong understanding of the market, and a commitment to innovation, turning a simple idea into a thriving business is not just possible—it's a journey worth pursuing.

CHAPTER VIII

Generating Business Ideas

Generating and Evaluating Business Ideas: From Creativity to Practicality

The foundation of every successful business begins with a strong idea—one that meets a market need, offers a unique solution, or improves upon existing products and services. However, coming up with a viable business concept requires more than just inspiration; it demands creativity, strategic thinking, and an understanding of market dynamics. Several methods can help entrepreneurs generate and refine business ideas, ensuring they are both innovative and feasible.

How to Generate Business Ideas

Creativity thrives when there is an open flow of ideas. Some of the most effective ways to generate business concepts include:

Brainstorming: Unlocking Creativity

One of the most common techniques for idea generation is brainstorming—a free-flowing process where individuals or groups propose ideas based on their experiences and observations. This method encourages out-of-the-box thinking, allowing unconventional and innovative ideas to emerge. The goal is not to critique or filter ideas initially but to generate as many possibilities as possible. Once a broad set of ideas is collected, they can be refined and assessed for feasibility.

Focus Groups: Gathering Valuable Insights

Focus groups involve structured discussions with potential customers or industry experts to gain insights into specific market needs. These conversations help refine initial business ideas by validating assumptions and identifying pain points that need to be addressed. Whether it's testing a new product concept or exploring industry trends, focus groups offer a deeper understanding of what the target audience truly wants.

Problem Inventory Analysis: Identifying Market Gaps

Rather than starting with a product or service in mind, another effective approach is to analyze existing problems and look for gaps in the market. By asking critical questions—such as whether similar ideas have been attempted before, the financial feasibility of the concept, and its long-term potential—entrepreneurs can identify opportunities that others might have overlooked. This inquiry-based approach ensures that the idea is both necessary and practical before investing time and resources into development.

Evaluating Business Ideas: Filtering the Best Concepts

Once several ideas are on the table, the next step is evaluation. Choosing the right idea requires a structured assessment to determine which concept has the highest potential for success. Here are some key methods used to evaluate business ideas:

Quick Screening with Pass-Fail Evaluation

A simple yet effective method is the pass-fail evaluation, where each idea is initially assessed against essential criteria such as timeline, budget, and alignment with business objectives. If an idea meets these basic requirements, it moves forward for deeper analysis. This method helps quickly eliminate ideas that are unrealistic or misaligned with available resources.

Structured Decision-Making with an Evaluation Matrix

For a more detailed assessment, an evaluation matrix can be used. Decision-makers assign scores to each idea based on specific factors like feasibility, innovation, and market demand. Along with numeric ratings, qualitative feedback is provided to highlight strengths and weaknesses. The overall score helps prioritize ideas and identify the most promising ones.

Comprehensive Analysis with SWOT Assessment

A SWOT (Strengths, Weaknesses, Opportunities, and Threats) analysis provides a well-rounded perspective on each idea. Strengths highlight the advantages of the concept, while weaknesses reveal potential challenges. Opportunities explore areas for growth, and threats examine external risks. This method is especially useful for long-term strategic planning, helping entrepreneurs anticipate challenges and prepare solutions in advance.

Comparing Ideas with Pairwise Analysis

Pairwise analysis is a direct comparison method where ideas are ranked or compared against each other based on set criteria. This approach is particularly useful when multiple strong ideas exist, as it helps determine which concept holds the most promise in terms of profitability, ease of implementation, and market demand.

Assessing Financial Viability with Financial Analysis

Beyond creativity and feasibility, a business idea must also be financially viable. Conducting a financial analysis using metrics like Return on Investment (ROI) and Net Present Value (NPV) can help determine whether an idea is worth pursuing. Understanding profit margins, projected expenses, and revenue potential ensures that decisions are grounded in financial reality, reducing the risk of investing in an unprofitable venture.

Turning an Idea into a Business

Generating a business idea is only the beginning. The real challenge lies in refining, validating, and executing that idea effectively. By using structured evaluation methods, entrepreneurs can eliminate weak concepts and focus on those with the highest potential.

A well-developed business idea aligns with market needs, personal strengths, and long-term financial sustainability. With the right approach, entrepreneurs can confidently move forward, turning an initial spark of inspiration into a thriving, successful venture.

CHAPTER IX

Sources of Entrepreneurial Opportunities

Where Do Business Ideas Come From? Recognizing Entrepreneurial Opportunities

Great business ideas don't appear out of thin air—they emerge from experience, observation, and an understanding of gaps in the market. Entrepreneurs who stay curious, proactive, and open to new possibilities are more likely to spot opportunities that others overlook. Business concepts can come from personal passions, professional expertise, external trends, or even frustrations with existing products and services. The key is recognizing where a need exists and finding a way to fill it.

Finding Business Inspiration

Turning Personal Interests into Profitable Ventures

Many successful businesses begin as passion projects. When an entrepreneur turns a hobby or personal interest into a business, they bring an inherent enthusiasm and deep knowledge to their venture. A photographer may start a creative studio, a fitness enthusiast may launch a coaching service, and a home baker might open an online pastry shop. By aligning a business with personal passions, the work becomes more fulfilling, and the chances of success increase.

Leveraging Work Experience and Industry Knowledge

Years of working in a particular industry can provide valuable insights into gaps in the market. Employees often notice inefficiencies, unmet customer needs, or outdated processes that could be improved. A software engineer might recognize the limitations of existing technology and develop a more efficient solution. A healthcare professional could identify gaps in patient care and introduce a new service model. When entrepreneurs apply their expertise to real-world problems, they create businesses that are both relevant and innovative.

Improving Existing Products and Services

Innovation doesn't always mean inventing something completely new. Many businesses are built by improving existing products or services. A frequent user of a product might notice flaws or areas for enhancement, inspiring them to create a better version. Alternatively, exposure to unfamiliar industries can spark fresh ideas—something as simple as experiencing a product or service in another country could inspire an entrepreneur to bring it to a new market.

Identifying Trends and Market Shifts

External changes—whether technological advancements, cultural shifts, economic conditions, or regulatory updates—can create powerful business opportunities. The rise of digital platforms, the demand for eco-friendly products, or changes in consumer behavior often lead to the emergence of new industries. Entrepreneurs who stay ahead of trends and understand how markets evolve can position themselves as pioneers in emerging fields.

Products vs. Services: Choosing the Right Business Model

One of the fundamental decisions entrepreneurs face is whether to sell a product, offer a service, or combine both. Each approach comes with distinct advantages and challenges, and choosing the right one depends on factors such as time, costs, and long-term scalability.

Selling Products: Advantages and Challenges

Physical or digital products allow customers to see, evaluate, and purchase with confidence. Immediate transactions mean faster revenue generation, but inventory management can be complex. Keeping products in stock, handling storage requirements, and managing supply chain logistics all add to the operational workload.

A major risk in product-based businesses is unsold inventory—perishable goods, in particular, can result in significant financial losses. Entrepreneurs must carefully plan production, anticipate demand, and ensure they have efficient distribution channels to avoid overstocking or stockouts.

Providing Services: Flexibility with Unique Challenges

Service-based businesses generally require lower startup costs and can be launched quickly. Unlike products, services do not require physical inventory, making them more accessible to new entrepreneurs. However, building customer trust is crucial—clients need to believe in the provider's expertise and reliability before making a purchase decision.

One of the biggest challenges in service businesses is scalability. Since services are delivered in real-time, business growth is often tied to the entrepreneur's availability. Expanding a service-based business may require hiring more professionals, automating processes, or offering digital services that allow for broader reach without significantly increasing costs.

Scaling and Sustaining a Business

Regardless of whether an entrepreneur chooses a product- or service-based model, long-term success requires careful planning, market awareness, and adaptability.

- Scalability Matters: Some products—such as software, online courses, or e-books—can be sold repeatedly without additional costs, making them highly scalable. Services, on the other hand, typically require increased resources as demand grows. However, certain services can scale if they transition into digital offerings or subscription models.
- Managing Stock and Supply Chains: A product-based business must balance supply and demand. Running out

of stock can frustrate customers, while excess inventory can lead to financial strain. Businesses must maintain a smooth supply chain to stay competitive.

- Sales and Marketing Are Key: Even the best products and services won't sell themselves. Entrepreneurs must develop effective sales strategies, optimize distribution channels, and continually assess pricing and marketing efforts to remain relevant in a competitive market.
- Staying Legally Compliant: Ensuring that products and services meet industry regulations is essential. Entrepreneurs must regularly review legal requirements to avoid compliance issues that could harm their business.

Building a Business That Lasts

Success in entrepreneurship isn't just about choosing between products or services—it's about understanding market needs, staying adaptable, and consistently delivering value to customers. Whether launching a passion project, leveraging professional expertise, or capitalizing on market trends, entrepreneurs who remain flexible and proactive are best positioned for long-term growth.

By carefully evaluating the right business model and keeping scalability in mind, any aspiring entrepreneur can create a venture that is not only profitable but also sustainable. The key is to stay informed, anticipate challenges, and continuously refine the business to meet evolving customer demands.

CHAPTER X

Identifying Market Opportunities

Building a successful business requires a deep understanding of the market—either by filling an existing gap or creating demand for a new product or service. Whether it's through innovation, improving current offerings, or introducing a unique approach, businesses thrive by meeting customer needs in ways others haven't.

Finding Market Gaps: Spotting Hidden Opportunities

One of the most effective ways to launch a successful business is by identifying gaps in the market. This means looking for unmet needs, inefficiencies, or areas where existing solutions fall short. It could involve developing a product that doesn't yet exist, refining an established service, or offering a fresh perspective that enhances customer satisfaction.

Understanding market gaps requires research, observation, and engagement. Analyzing customer behavior, studying competitor weaknesses, and gathering insights from industry trends can reveal lucrative opportunities. However, just because a product or service is missing from the market doesn't automatically mean there's demand for it. Sometimes, past attempts have failed due to lack of interest, high costs, or logistical challenges. Thorough research helps determine whether a gap is a genuine opportunity or a potential pitfall.

Key Market Insights That Influence Success

- Competitive Markets: These industries are saturated with businesses offering similar products or services, meaning no single company dominates pricing.
- Demand Levels: The number of customers willing to pay for a product or service at a given price determines whether an idea is viable.
- Market Disruptors: Innovative companies introduce new business models, products, or technologies that shake up industries and often become market leaders.

Standing Out in a Crowded Market

Competition is inevitable in any industry, but businesses that differentiate themselves have the best chance of thriving. The key to success lies in offering a unique value proposition that customers recognize and appreciate. This could be through innovation, superior quality, personalized service, or guarantees that build trust.

While pricing can be a competitive tool, relying solely on low prices can be risky. Instead, businesses should focus on creating long-term value, ensuring customers see the benefits of their offering beyond just cost savings. Monitoring competitors and adapting to changes is also essential to maintaining a market advantage.

Strategies for Gaining a Competitive Edge

- Differentiation: Offer unique benefits that set your brand apart. This could include features, experiences, or exceptional service that competitors can't match.
- Cost Efficiency Without Compromise: Competing on price is only effective when it doesn't sacrifice quality or long-term profitability.
- Balancing Value and Profitability: A business must deliver value to customers while ensuring sustainable profit margins.
- Continuous Market Monitoring: Keeping an eye on competitors and industry trends helps businesses adapt and refine their strategies.

Tapping Into Market Gaps for Business Growth

Focusing on underserved customer segments is a great way to grow a business. Certain groups may have limited access to suitable options, while emerging trends can create new opportunities. Conducting thorough market research can reveal whether your product or service meets an unfulfilled need, making it easier to position yourself effectively.

Choosing the Right Price-Quality Strategy

How a business positions its product in terms of price and quality affects its appeal to different customer segments.

- Premium (High Price, High Quality): Luxury items made with superior materials, such as fine leather goods, attract customers willing to pay for durability and craftsmanship.

- Affordable and Trend-Driven (Low Price, Low Quality): Budget-friendly fashion or disposable products cater to younger audiences looking for style over longevity.
- Mass Market Appeal (Medium Price, Low Quality): Trendy yet lower-durability products may attract a broad audience but could lead to customer dissatisfaction.

Positioning a New Product or Service for Maximum Impact

For a business to gain traction, its offering must be memorable, practical, and valuable. A well-positioned product should strike the right balance between affordability, quality, and broad appeal. Some key attributes that contribute to strong positioning include:

- Visually Appealing and Trendy: A product that looks good often gains attention faster.
- Reasonable Pricing: Customers seek value—something that isn't too expensive but doesn't seem cheap.
- Durability and Reliability: Products should meet expectations for quality, ensuring repeat purchases.
- Broad Demographic Appeal: Businesses that cater to multiple age groups and preferences have a larger potential customer base.
- Clear Value Proposition: Customers should immediately understand why a product is worth buying.

Building a Sustainable Competitive Advantage

A strong market position isn't achieved overnight. It requires constant evaluation, refinement, and strategic planning. Businesses that consistently deliver value, stay adaptable, and innovate remain competitive in the long run.

By understanding market demand, pricing strategies, and customer expectations, entrepreneurs can make informed decisions that lead to sustainable success. Whether by addressing unmet needs, improving existing solutions, or introducing a breakthrough innovation, the businesses that truly understand their customers will always have the upper hand.

CHAPTER XI

What Makes Your Business Stand Out?

Defining Your Business Identity: Standing Out in a Competitive Market

In today's crowded business landscape, clearly communicating what makes your business unique is essential. Your value proposition should not only highlight the benefits your customers can expect but also differentiate your offerings from competitors. Whether through innovation, superior quality, outstanding service, or competitive pricing, your ability to stand out will determine your success.

Creating a Strong Competitive Advantage

Understanding your customers' evolving needs is key to staying relevant. The strategies that set you apart today may need refinement in the future as new competitors emerge and market demands shift. To maintain a strong position, businesses must:

- Continuously analyze and refine their Unique Selling Propositions (USPs) to ensure they remain relevant.
- Monitor competitors and identify ways to improve upon their strengths and weaknesses.
- Evaluate the cost-effectiveness of their USPs to maintain healthy profit margins.

- Stay ahead of market trends and anticipate customer expectations.

Developing a Unique Selling Proposition (USP)

Your USP is the defining feature that makes customers choose your business over others. Differentiation can come in many forms:

- Product Uniqueness: Offer something distinct—better quality, improved safety, or innovative design.
- Exclusive Services: Provide a level of service that competitors cannot match, whether it's exceptional customer support, personalized experiences, or added convenience.
- Balanced Pricing Strategy: While competitive pricing can be an advantage, it should never come at the cost of quality or long-term profitability. Customers assess both price and value before making purchasing decisions.

By clearly articulating your business's unique benefits, you not only attract customers but also build brand loyalty and trust.

Clarifying Your Business Goals: Laying a Strong Foundation

A successful business isn't just about making sales—it's about having a clear vision and direction. Defining your purpose, values, and mission provides the framework for decision-making, strategy, and brand identity.

Defining Your Purpose

Your business purpose should serve as a guiding principle, shaping your goals and long-term vision. Whether it's about innovation, customer satisfaction, or social impact, having a clear sense of purpose helps in creating a business that is both sustainable and fulfilling.

Establishing Core Values

Your business values should reflect what you stand for—whether it's honesty, innovation, customer-first service, or sustainability. These values should be embedded in your business culture and communicated to employees, partners, and customers. For example, a travel agency catering to retirees might emphasize trust, quality, comfort, and adventure, ensuring that all aspects of its services align with these principles.

Crafting a Mission Statement

A mission statement serves as a concise summary of your business's purpose. It should answer three key questions:

- What? What products or services do you provide?
- Who? Who is your target audience?
- How? How do you meet customer needs effectively?

Alongside your mission statement, you can create a vision statement, which outlines where you see your business in the future, and a values statement, which highlights the core principles guiding your operations.

Why Your Mission Statement Matters

A well-crafted mission statement is more than just words—it's a motivational tool for your team and a marketing asset that conveys your business's identity to customers. However, credibility comes not just from saying the right things but from demonstrating them through actions. Customers and employees alike value businesses that live up to their promises.

Choosing the Right Business Structure

Selecting the right business structure is a crucial decision that impacts everything from legal responsibilities to financial stability and growth potential. Whether you're starting alone, with a partner, or planning to expand in the future, understanding your options helps you make an informed choice.

Evaluating Your Options

The best structure for your business depends on:

- Complexity: How much administrative and legal work are you prepared to handle?
- Risk and Liability: Do you want to separate personal assets from business liabilities?
- Growth Potential: Are you starting small with plans to scale, or do you need external funding?

Many businesses begin as sole proprietorships or partnerships, but as they grow, transitioning to a limited liability structure can offer greater protection and easier access to financing.

Types of Business Structures

1. Sole Proprietorship

    - Pros: Easy setup, full control, and profits taxed as personal income.
    - Cons: Unlimited liability (business debts are personal debts), limited funding options, and business lifespan tied to the owner.

2. Partnership

    - Similar to a sole proprietorship but with shared resources and risks.
    - Limited Partnership: Some partners have limited liability, while one retains full responsibility.

3. Corporation

    - Private Company: A business with limited shareholders and fewer legal formalities, requiring minimum capital investment.
    - Public Company: A larger entity that can raise funds through public investment, subject to stricter legal and financial regulations.

4. Franchising

    - Involves operating a business under an established brand's name, benefiting from its reputation and support systems.

- ◦ While franchisees operate independently, they must adhere to the franchisor's business model and agreements.

Making the Right Choice

As businesses evolve, their legal structure may need to change to accommodate growth, attract investors, or limit personal risk. Understanding the benefits and challenges of each structure helps in making a decision that aligns with long-term business goals.

Building a Business with Purpose and Strength

Success in business is about more than just offering a product or service—it's about creating value, defining your purpose, and making strategic decisions that ensure sustainability.

By:

- Developing a strong USP that differentiates your business,
- Clarifying your mission and values to guide your strategy,
- Choosing the right business structure to protect your assets and support growth,

You position your business for long-term success. With a clear vision and a well-structured approach, any entrepreneur can build a thriving, competitive, and purpose-driven business.

CHAPTER XII

Business Plans

Creating a Business Plan: A Roadmap to Success

A well-structured business plan is the backbone of any successful venture. It serves as both a strategic guide for internal decision-making and a persuasive tool for securing funding. By outlining clear goals, analyzing the market, and presenting realistic financial projections, a business plan provides direction and increases the likelihood of long-term success.

Understanding the Business Plan Process

Before drafting a business plan, thorough market research is essential. Identifying market opportunities, understanding customer needs, and defining a competitive edge help create a solid foundation. The plan should also include realistic financial projections, offering investors and lenders a clear view of the business's path to profitability.

When presenting the plan, clarity is key. The executive summary should be concise—ideally no more than two pages—and written in simple, direct language. Avoiding unnecessary jargon makes the plan accessible to a wider audience, ensuring that stakeholders quickly grasp its core message.

Why a Business Plan Matters

Many entrepreneurs overlook the importance of a business plan, but it is a crucial tool for success. It ensures that no critical element is missed, from securing funding to operational strategy. By estimating costs and revenue projections accurately, entrepreneurs can determine financial viability and attract potential investors.

A well-written plan also highlights areas where outside expertise may be required, whether in marketing, accounting, or operations. Additionally, conducting market research as part of the planning process offers valuable insights into customer preferences and competitor strategies, strengthening a business's competitive position.

Choosing the Right Business Model

One of the most critical decisions in launching a startup is selecting a business model—the framework that defines how the business generates revenue and operates efficiently. A strong business model not only delivers value to customers but also ensures long-term profitability.

Understanding Different Business Models

Businesses operate in different ways depending on their market, product, and long-term vision. Some rely on direct customer interaction, while others leverage technology or distribution networks to scale their operations.

Retail and E-Commerce Models

Traditional retail businesses sell products through physical stores, while e-commerce has revolutionized sales by enabling businesses to reach customers online. Many businesses now use a hybrid approach, integrating both physical and digital storefronts to maximize customer convenience.

Production and Distribution Models

Manufacturers create goods from raw materials and distribute them to wholesalers or retailers, ensuring products reach end consumers efficiently. In contrast, direct sales bypass intermediaries, allowing businesses to engage with customers one-on-one. Franchising enables individuals to operate under an established brand, benefiting from its recognition and proven systems.

Service-Based and Subscription Models

Some businesses focus on services rather than physical products. Agencies and brokerages connect buyers and sellers, earning commissions for their role in facilitating transactions. Others, like streaming platforms and fitness centers, adopt a subscription model, offering continuous access to services for a recurring fee.

Innovative Revenue Models

The freemium model allows businesses to attract users with a free basic offering while charging for premium features. Affiliate marketing generates income by promoting third-party products, earning commissions from resulting sales. Advertising-driven businesses create content to attract audiences, then sell ad space to other companies. Licensing enables businesses to commercialize intellectual property, earning royalties without directly producing physical goods.

Building a Sustainable Business Model

A successful business model is not just about making sales—it must be scalable, adaptable, and customer-focused. Many companies blend multiple models to maximize profitability. A digital magazine, for example, may combine a subscription model for exclusive content with advertising revenue from sponsored partnerships. Similarly, a software company might offer freemium access, encouraging users to upgrade to paid versions for additional features.

When refining a business model, several factors come into play. Understanding customer preferences helps shape the user experience, while staying informed about market trends ensures businesses remain competitive. Operational feasibility determines whether a model is practical given available resources, and scalability assesses the business's potential to grow without a proportional increase in costs.

Laying the Foundation for Long-Term Success

Launching a business isn't just about having a great idea—it's about strategic planning, execution, and adaptability. A business plan acts as a roadmap, ensuring that goals, financial strategies, and operational plans are clearly defined. A strong business model supports sustainable growth, while the ability to pivot in response to market changes sets apart businesses that last from those that fade.

By making informed choices from the outset, entrepreneurs can minimize risks, attract investors, and build ventures that withstand the test of time. Success is not just about starting strong—it's about continuously evolving to meet new challenges and opportunities in an ever-changing business landscape.

CHAPTER XIII

Business Strategy

Developing a Business Strategy: Laying the Foundation for Success

A well-defined business strategy is essential for identifying opportunities, addressing challenges, and establishing a clear path to success. It acts as a blueprint that outlines business goals, market positioning, and financial planning, ensuring that each step is intentional and aligned with long-term objectives.

One of the most critical aspects of strategy development is the creation of a comprehensive business plan. This document serves as both an internal guide and an external tool for securing funding. While preparing a business plan may take several weeks, its importance cannot be overstated. A well-structured plan provides clarity, helps anticipate potential risks, and offers investors and stakeholders a realistic projection of financial outcomes.

Structuring a Business Plan: Essential Components

When drafting a business plan, maintaining clarity and conciseness is key. The executive summary should be straightforward and limited to two pages, ensuring that technical terms are explained in simple language for easy comprehension. Studies suggest that nearly 69% of small business owners believe that having a structured business plan significantly contributes to success, underscoring its role in sustainable growth.

Executive Summary: A Snapshot of the Business

As the first section investors and decision-makers review, the executive summary should be persuasive yet concise, providing a strong overview of the company. It includes details on business structure, the product or service offered, and the target customer profile. Setting clear short-term and long-term objectives ensures direction, with defined goals spanning one, three, and five years. Financial projections, including expected sales, costs, and funding requirements, should also be highlighted.

A well-crafted executive summary often serves as an elevator pitch—a two-minute introduction designed to capture attention and spark interest.

Products and Services: Defining What the Business Offers

A business plan should provide a comprehensive breakdown of the products or services being offered. If a product is newly developed, visuals or prototypes can help illustrate its functionality and appeal. Businesses with multiple offerings should highlight how their range of products or services complements one another. It is crucial to establish what differentiates the product or service from competitors—whether through innovation, superior quality, or added value.

Crafting an Effective Marketing Strategy

Marketing plays a pivotal role in business success, requiring well-defined strategies to reach and retain customers. The primary marketing channels should be identified, including social media platforms, company websites, and additional promotional methods such as email campaigns and content marketing. A combination of digital and traditional approaches often yields the best results, ensuring visibility and engagement across different audience segments.

Business Background and Team Expertise

Investors and stakeholders often assess the experience and qualifications of the team behind the business. Highlighting relevant industry experience, past accomplishments, and key connections adds credibility. Any certifications or degrees relevant to the business, such as a background in horticulture for a gardening service, should also be mentioned. Additionally, outlining any ongoing or planned training programs, particularly in leadership or business management, demonstrates a commitment to professional growth.

Understanding the Market: Customer and Competitive Analysis

Market research forms the backbone of a business plan, offering insights into target audiences, consumer behavior, and industry trends. A well-defined customer profile should outline whether the business serves individuals, corporate clients, or a niche demographic. Local, national, or international market potential must be considered, supported by research on demand and competitive positioning.

A thorough competitor analysis helps identify strengths, weaknesses, and areas for differentiation. Understanding competitors' pricing, product quality, and market approach enables businesses to carve out a unique space. Conducting a SWOT analysis—evaluating strengths, weaknesses, opportunities, and threats—provides further clarity on where a business stands and what strategies can be implemented to mitigate risks.

Differentiation is key in any competitive market. Businesses must clearly define their Unique Selling Proposition (USP)—the feature or service that sets them apart. Whether it's faster delivery, eco-friendly options, or an exclusive product line, the USP should be compelling enough to attract and retain customers.

Setting Pricing and Managing Costs

A solid pricing strategy determines profitability while ensuring customer satisfaction. The cost of production, delivery expenses, and profit margins must all be carefully calculated. Understanding how much customers are willing to pay and ensuring that pricing reflects product value without being prohibitive is essential for long-term sustainability.

Operations and Logistics: Managing Day-to-Day Business Functions

The operational structure of a business determines how efficiently it functions. A plan should outline logistics, from supply chain management to equipment and resource allocation. This includes sourcing materials, maintaining inventory, and establishing smooth delivery channels. Legal compliance, payment processing, and insurance considerations must also be factored into operations.

Financial Planning and Future Projections

Financial projections offer a realistic assessment of expected revenue, operating costs, and overall profitability. A well-structured business plan should include sales forecasts, taking into account seasonal variations and market fluctuations. Tracking cash flow projections allows businesses to maintain stability and adjust strategies when necessary.

Preparing for Uncertainties: Contingency and Exit Strategies

Unforeseen challenges are an inevitable part of business operations. Developing a contingency plan ensures that setbacks can be managed effectively, whether through cost reductions, alternative revenue streams, or adjusting business models.

Long-term planning might include shifting from a physical storefront to an online model or adapting to industry changes. Short-term adjustments, such as temporary cost-cutting measures or promotional efforts to boost sales, can also be outlined. An exit strategy, while not often considered early on, is useful for businesses looking at potential mergers, acquisitions, or even responsible closure if necessary. Documenting lessons learned and skills acquired during the business journey ensures that knowledge can be leveraged in future ventures.

Building a Sustainable and Scalable Business

A business plan is more than just a document—it's a dynamic tool that evolves alongside the company. It provides a clear direction, ensures financial preparedness, and strengthens decision-making processes. The ability to adapt to market changes, refine strategies, and scale operations sets thriving businesses apart from those that struggle.

Success is not just about having a great product or service—it is about strategic execution, informed decision-making, and a willingness to evolve. By investing time and effort into planning, businesses position themselves for long-term growth, investor confidence, and resilience in an ever-changing marketplace.

CHAPTER XIV

Defining Your Business

Defining Your Business: Crafting a Clear and Effective Strategy

A well-defined business strategy serves as a foundation for success, providing clarity on long-term goals and the steps needed to achieve them. Developing a strong strategy involves thorough research, input from stakeholders, and a clear sense of purpose. By defining the direction of your business early on, you ensure alignment between your objectives, market opportunities, and operational capabilities.

Establishing Your Mission and Vision

A mission statement is the core of any business strategy, outlining the fundamental purpose of the company and the value it offers. It serves as a guiding principle, influencing decision-making and shaping future growth. A well-crafted mission statement should answer why the business exists, who it serves, and what problems it solves. This clarity ensures that all business activities align with the long-term vision.

To create a strong market presence, businesses must go beyond just defining their purpose. Understanding strengths, weaknesses, opportunities, and threats through a SWOT analysis allows entrepreneurs to build resilience and adaptability. Leveraging competitive strategies—such as superior quality, exceptional customer service, or unique offerings—helps differentiate a business from competitors and establishes a strong market position.

Evaluating Strategic Options

A business strategy should be both ambitious and realistic. While setting long-term goals, it is essential to ensure they align with what is feasible in the given market environment. The target audience should match the business's objectives, and all potential strategies must be assessed for viability. Comparing different approaches and competitive strategies allows businesses to refine their direction and make well-informed decisions.

Since business environments evolve, a strategy should never remain static. External factors such as economic shifts, new regulations, and technological advancements can impact operations, requiring regular reviews and adjustments. Staying informed about market trends and industry changes ensures that businesses remain competitive and adaptable.

Competing Effectively in the Market

Success in business often depends on how well a company differentiates itself. Competitive strategies revolve around perceived value, unique offerings, and superior customer service, allowing businesses to build brand loyalty and attract a steady customer base.

One approach to gaining a competitive edge is by enhancing customer convenience. Businesses that offer localized services, flexible hours, or personalized experiences create deeper connections with their audience.

Whether it's a retail store extending its operating hours or a service provider tailoring solutions to individual client needs, these personalized touches build strong relationships and encourage repeat business.

Another way to stand out is by offering unique products or services that are difficult to replicate. Businesses that cater to niche markets or develop specialized offerings can create exclusivity, making it harder for competitors to compete on the same level. Customization, premium quality, and specialized expertise can all contribute to creating an unmatchable value proposition.

Customer service also plays a crucial role in competitive strategy. Businesses that prioritize seamless transactions, personalized support, and flexible policies cultivate strong customer relationships. Offering installment payment options, hassle-free returns, or concierge-style service enhances the overall experience and encourages customer loyalty.

Understanding the Market and Business Models

Choosing the right market approach is key to long-term sustainability. Businesses can target mass markets, specialized niches, or a mix of both, depending on their goals and capabilities. The choice of market influences branding, pricing, and distribution strategies.

Mass-market businesses aim to reach a wide audience and rely on high-volume sales and broad appeal. This model often involves substantial marketing efforts but offers the advantage of economies of scale. Well-known brands like Coca-Cola, Apple, and Nike follow this approach, ensuring their products appeal to a diverse customer base.

For businesses catering to individual consumers, the B2C (Business to Consumer) model is common. These businesses focus on emotional connections, convenience, and brand loyalty to drive sales. Companies like Amazon and Uber excel in this space by offering seamless shopping experiences and user-friendly platforms that cater to modern consumer needs.

In contrast, the B2B (Business to Business) model involves transactions between companies, often characterized by longer sales cycles and higher order values. Businesses operating in this space provide solutions tailored to corporate needs, such as software providers serving enterprises or manufacturers supplying raw materials to industrial clients.

A hybrid model, B2B2C (Business to Business to Consumer), bridges the gap between businesses and end consumers. In this setup, one business sells products to another, which then markets them to customers. A common example is a clothing manufacturer supplying a retail chain, which then sells the items to shoppers. This approach allows businesses to scale while leveraging the marketing reach of their partners.

For businesses that cater to niche markets, success lies in specialization and differentiation. Rather than competing on volume, niche businesses focus on offering tailored solutions that justify higher price points. Whether it's sustainable products, handcrafted goods, or specialized consulting services, niche markets attract customers looking for highly specific, high-value offerings.

Choosing the Right Model for Your Business

The decision to operate as B2C, B2B, or B2B2C depends on the nature of the product or service, target customers, and overall market strategy. Some businesses integrate multiple models to maximize revenue potential. A technology company, for instance, may sell software directly to individual users while also licensing it to corporate clients.

Understanding market dynamics and selecting the most suitable business model is essential for ensuring growth, scalability, and profitability. Businesses that recognize where they fit in the broader landscape can optimize operations and tailor marketing efforts to reach the right audience.

Laying the Groundwork for Long-Term Success

A strong business strategy is built on clarity, adaptability, and informed decision-making. By defining objectives, identifying competitive advantages, and selecting the right business model, entrepreneurs create a roadmap for sustainable growth.

Success is not solely about entering the market—it's about staying ahead, evolving with industry trends, and continuously refining the approach. Businesses that invest in strategy development, market research, and customer engagement position themselves for long-term profitability and industry leadership.

With a well-defined plan and a focus on execution, businesses can navigate challenges, capitalize on emerging opportunities, and build a brand that thrives in a competitive landscape.

CHAPTER XV

Customer Base

Understanding Your Customer Base: The Key to Business Success

Recognizing who your customers are is fundamental to building a thriving business. A clear understanding of their preferences, behaviors, and needs allows businesses to tailor their products and marketing strategies effectively, ensuring they reach the right audience through the most appropriate channels. By segmenting the market and creating detailed customer profiles, businesses can enhance engagement, optimize sales, and build lasting relationships with their audience.

Targeting the Right Customers

Every market is diverse, and customers have varying needs, expectations, and buying habits. To cater to these differences, businesses must identify specific customer segments and customize their offerings accordingly. Market segmentation is a structured approach to dividing customers into groups based on shared characteristics, allowing businesses to focus on those most likely to benefit from their products or services.

Segmenting the Market: Understanding Customer Differences

Market segmentation involves categorizing customers based on demographics, geography, psychographics, and behavior. Each of these factors provides valuable insights that businesses can use to craft targeted marketing campaigns and personalized services.

Demographic Segmentation: Who Your Customers Are

Demographic factors help create a detailed customer profile by identifying fundamental characteristics that influence purchasing decisions. Businesses often analyze age, gender, marital status, ethnicity, income, and occupation to tailor their offerings.

Age plays a significant role, as younger generations may favor technology-driven products, while older consumers may prefer traditional services. Gender-specific preferences influence industries like fashion, cosmetics, and fitness. Marital status can shape buying behavior, with single individuals and families having different spending priorities. Cultural influences affect food, clothing, and entertainment choices, while income and occupation determine purchasing power and the need for specialized products.

For instance, a luxury brand might target high-income individuals, while a fast-food chain would appeal to a wider audience with varying price points.

Geographic Segmentation: Where Your Customers Are

Location-based segmentation tailors products and services to customers' specific regional and environmental needs.

Businesses adjust their strategies based on whether they operate in urban, suburban, or rural areas, recognizing the different demands in each setting. Climate plays a significant role, with winter apparel brands focusing on colder regions and air conditioning companies targeting warmer climates.

Understanding local preferences also helps businesses adapt their offerings to cultural differences. A global brand may customize its menu to suit regional tastes, just as a retail store might stock items based on the preferences of local shoppers.

Psychographic Segmentation: What Drives Customer Choices

Beyond tangible factors like age and location, customer personalities, values, and lifestyles significantly influence buying behavior. Psychographic segmentation focuses on how people think, feel, and act, providing deeper insights into their motivations.

Consumer interests and hobbies shape product preferences, while values—such as sustainability or luxury appeal—affect purchasing decisions. A company offering organic products may attract environmentally conscious consumers, while a luxury watch brand would appeal to those who value status and exclusivity. Social media habits also play a role, as businesses tailor engagement strategies based on whether their audience prefers platforms like Instagram, LinkedIn, or TikTok.

Behavioral Segmentation: How Customers Interact with Brands

Understanding purchasing behavior allows businesses to target customers more effectively. Some buyers are loyal to specific brands, while others make decisions based on price, availability, or convenience. Businesses can use behavioral segmentation to create loyalty programs for frequent buyers, offer discounts to attract price-sensitive shoppers, or personalize promotions based on customer engagement history.

Shopping preferences also vary, with some customers preferring in-store experiences while others rely entirely on e-commerce platforms. The way customers interact with brands—whether they buy based on necessity, impulse, or extensive research—determines how marketing efforts should be structured.

For example, an electronics retailer might target tech enthusiasts with early-bird discounts, while a fashion brand could release exclusive collections for repeat customers to reward loyalty.

Bringing Customer Insights to Life

To better understand potential customers, businesses can create customer avatars or personas—detailed profiles representing different customer types. These personas help businesses visualize their target audience and design marketing strategies that cater specifically to their needs.

Developing customer avatars involves research techniques such as analyzing competitor social media pages, reading industry blogs, and identifying key influencers in the field. By gathering insights into customer behavior and preferences, businesses can refine their messaging, product offerings, and service approaches.

A structured approach to customer segmentation ensures that marketing efforts are directed at the most promising potential customers, avoiding wasted resources on the wrong audience. Businesses that deeply understand their customers can craft strategies that resonate, leading to higher engagement, increased sales, and stronger brand loyalty.

The Power of Knowing Your Market

A business that truly understands its customers is well-positioned for long-term success. By segmenting the market effectively and tailoring strategies to meet specific consumer needs, companies can enhance customer satisfaction, improve brand positioning, and drive sustainable growth. Whether through demographic analysis, geographic targeting, psychographic insights, or behavioral tracking, businesses that listen to and respond to their audience will always stay ahead of the competition.

By adopting a customer-first approach, businesses not only build stronger relationships but also create products and services that genuinely add value, ensuring their continued relevance in an ever-changing marketplace.

CHAPTER XVI

Valuating Business Demand

Evaluating Market Demand: Ensuring Business Viability

Enthusiasm for a business idea is important, but it must be balanced with objective research to determine whether there is sufficient demand for a product or service. A great idea alone is not enough—understanding customer needs, market trends, and competitor performance is essential for success. By conducting thorough research, testing concepts, and refining ideas, businesses can make informed decisions that increase their chances of sustainability and profitability.

Clarifying the Business Idea

Before assessing demand, it is crucial to clearly define the product or service and identify the target audience. A successful business needs a well-defined customer base that is large enough to support growth and sustainability. Factors such as location—whether local, national, or global—play a role in determining accessibility and potential reach.

Understanding the competitive landscape is also vital. Businesses must assess existing competitors, their offerings, pricing, and market positioning. A direct competitor may pose a challenge, but differentiation in terms of quality, pricing, or unique selling points can create a competitive advantage. Analyzing customer expectations and industry trends helps businesses refine their value propositions and better align with market needs.

Determining Market Demand

Once the business concept is clear, the next step is to analyze demand. A product or service must attract a stable and reliable customer base to be viable. Demand should remain steady over time, though fluctuations due to seasonality or trends should be accounted for in financial planning.

Pricing is another key consideration. A business must strike a balance between affordability and profitability, ensuring that customers are willing to pay for the product or service at a sustainable price point. If the market is saturated with similar offerings, businesses need to evaluate how they can differentiate themselves to retain customers and build a loyal following.

Studying competitors' successes and failures provides valuable insights. If similar businesses are thriving, it indicates demand; if they are struggling, it may signal an issue in the market that needs further investigation. Understanding what works and what doesn't allows for better decision-making and strategy development.

Refining the Business Idea Based on Research

Market research plays a pivotal role in refining an idea before launching a business. Gathering industry insights, consumer preferences, and competitive data ensures that products and services align with actual demand.

Desk research is an effective starting point. Analyzing industry reports, customer reviews, and statistical data provides a broad view of market trends and consumer behavior. Online sources, government publications, and business forums offer valuable information at little to no cost.

Speaking with industry experts and business professionals is another way to gain practical insights. Attending trade shows, networking events, and online industry discussions allows entrepreneurs to engage with those who have firsthand experience in the market. Learning from established businesses helps in avoiding common pitfalls and adopting successful strategies.

Gathering direct customer feedback through surveys and social media engagement is essential. Tools such as Google Forms, SurveyMonkey, and social media polls enable businesses to assess potential customer interest and preferences. Simple questionnaires targeting different consumer segments help validate the business idea and uncover potential improvements.

Once feedback is collected, adjustments should be made based on findings. If early responses indicate a lack of interest or highlight specific concerns, modifications may be necessary. Being open to change and adapting to customer needs ensures that the business is aligned with market demand.

Testing the Idea: Gathering Real-World Insights

Before committing to a full-scale launch, testing the product or service on a small scale can help validate its viability. A pilot phase allows businesses to refine their approach and make necessary adjustments based on real customer experiences.

A small test group of potential customers can provide invaluable insights. Offering limited samples, trial services, or early access at discounted rates helps gauge interest and identify areas for improvement. If launching a service such as coaching or consulting, offering short sessions or introductory packages can reveal whether there is demand and what aspects need refinement.

Collecting direct feedback from test users is critical. Observing their reactions, asking about their experiences, and determining whether they would be willing to pay full price for the offering provides tangible evidence of demand. Positive responses suggest a viable opportunity, while lukewarm reactions indicate areas needing improvement.

Based on this feedback, businesses should refine their offerings again. Adjustments in pricing, features, or marketing approaches may be necessary to enhance appeal and increase the likelihood of long-term success.

Understanding Demand and Competitive Pressures

A business must exist within an ecosystem of supply and demand. While having a unique product or service is advantageous, its success ultimately depends on whether enough customers are willing to buy at a sustainable price. The number of competitors in the market and their performance can impact pricing structures and profitability.

Oversupply in a market can drive prices down, making it difficult for new businesses to enter profitably. In contrast, identifying gaps where demand is unmet allows businesses to position themselves strategically. Ensuring accessibility—both in terms of product availability and marketing reach—further enhances chances of success.

Ignoring market demand can lead to costly mistakes, forcing businesses to modify their strategies post-launch or even reconsider their offerings entirely. Continuous research and monitoring of consumer behavior help businesses stay ahead of trends, anticipate shifts, and make proactive adjustments.

Assessing and Adapting to Market Conditions

Assessing demand is not a one-time process. Consumer preferences, industry trends, and economic conditions are constantly evolving, making continuous research essential. Engaging with industry peers, tracking competitors, and monitoring consumer sentiment enable businesses to adapt and remain competitive.

During the planning stage, refining ideas based on market research and expert input minimizes risks. Ongoing evaluation ensures that businesses remain aligned with customer needs and market trends. Keeping a flexible approach allows for necessary adjustments, helping businesses thrive in changing environments.

Recognizing when an idea is not viable is just as important as refining one that has potential. If research and testing indicate a lack of demand, pivoting to a better opportunity or refining the approach can prevent losses. Being persistent but adaptable ensures that businesses move forward with ideas that have real market potential.

The Power of Informed Decision-Making

Success in business is not based on assumptions or enthusiasm alone—it requires a deep understanding of customer needs, market conditions, and competitive landscapes. Through thorough research, real-world testing, and strategic refinement, entrepreneurs can ensure they are entering a market with genuine demand.

By continuously assessing, refining, and adapting, businesses increase their chances of success, reduce financial risks, and position themselves for long-term growth. Making informed decisions at every stage of business development leads to stronger, more resilient enterprises that thrive in competitive environments.

CHAPTER XVII

Procuring Products and Supplies

Sourcing Supplies for Your Business: Balancing Cost, Quality, and Ethics

Choosing the right suppliers is a critical decision that influences product quality, operational efficiency, and business reputation. Whether sourcing locally or internationally, balancing cost, sustainability, and reliability ensures that your business maintains high standards while staying competitive. Understanding the advantages and challenges of different sourcing methods allows for strategic procurement that aligns with long-term business goals.

Factors to Consider When Procuring Supplies

Sourcing decisions depend on a range of factors, from budget constraints to ethical production standards. Each option—whether using recycled materials, local suppliers, national distributors, or international sources—comes with distinct benefits and challenges.

Reused or Repurposed Materials: Sustainable and Cost-Effective

Using recycled or repurposed materials reduces waste and lowers costs, making it an attractive option for businesses focused on sustainability. This approach supports environmental efforts by minimizing reliance on new raw materials. However, quality and availability can be inconsistent, making it challenging to maintain steady production. Ensuring that repurposed materials meet safety standards is crucial to avoid potential product defects or compliance issues.

Small, Local Suppliers: Community-Focused and Flexible

Sourcing from local businesses strengthens community ties, reduces transportation-related emissions, and provides opportunities for customization and personalized service. Working with local suppliers ensures a more transparent supply chain and builds long-term partnerships based on trust. However, local suppliers may have limited product ranges and higher costs due to smaller production scales. While this approach promotes economic sustainability, businesses must assess whether local sourcing meets all operational needs.

Major National Suppliers: Reliable and Scalable

Larger national suppliers offer competitive pricing, consistent stock availability, and streamlined logistics, making them a dependable choice for businesses with high-volume needs. These suppliers often have established shipping systems and return policies, reducing the complexities of procurement. However, national suppliers may have less flexibility in customizing products or adjusting to small business needs. Additionally, businesses relying on the same large suppliers may struggle with product differentiation, leading to increased competition within the same market.

International Sourcing: Expanding Options, Lowering Costs

Global sourcing provides access to specialized products and cost-effective materials, especially from countries with lower labor costs or abundant natural resources. This approach is useful for businesses requiring unique materials not readily available domestically. However, longer shipping times, fluctuating currency exchange rates, and potential import tariffs must be factored into procurement planning. Outsourcing quality control may also add an extra layer of complexity, requiring thorough vetting of international suppliers to maintain product consistency.

Key Considerations in Supplier Selection

Beyond cost and convenience, selecting the right supplier requires evaluating quality, reliability, sustainability, and ethical production standards. Businesses that balance affordability with responsible sourcing build stronger brand reputations and appeal to increasingly conscious consumers who value ethical production.

Ensuring that a supplier follows ethical labor practices and meets sustainability criteria enhances credibility. Many consumers now prefer businesses that source responsibly, making fair labor practices and environmentally friendly sourcing strong selling points. Transparency in supply chains is crucial, as unethical practices can harm a brand's reputation and consumer trust.

Reliability is another critical factor. Delays in supply chains affect inventory, disrupt production schedules, and impact customer satisfaction. Businesses should assess suppliers' track records in meeting deadlines and maintaining product quality.

Flexibility is also essential, particularly for businesses needing customized products or seasonal stock adjustments. Smaller suppliers or local manufacturers may offer greater adaptability, allowing businesses to refine product specifications based on customer preferences.

Making Informed Supplier Choices

Selecting suppliers impacts not just cost but also business efficiency and customer satisfaction. Evaluating potential suppliers through careful research helps businesses avoid procurement issues.

Comparing price, safety standards, product quality, and reliability allows businesses to determine whether to source directly from manufacturers or use third-party distributors. Industry trade shows, networking events, and supplier visits help in understanding supplier operations, material sourcing, and production capabilities.

When sourcing internationally, businesses must also account for language barriers and cultural differences that may lead to miscommunication. Clear agreements on product specifications, delivery schedules, and quality control measures are essential to avoid logistical complications.

Deciding Whether to Make, Reuse, or Buy

Some businesses may benefit from in-house production, especially when quality control is a priority. However, manufacturing in-house requires significant investment in equipment, training, and labor, which may not be feasible for startups or small businesses. In some cases, sourcing recycled or repurposed materials provides an ethical and cost-effective alternative to purchasing new supplies.

For businesses considering importing goods, securing proper licenses, assessing import duties, and understanding trading terms are essential. Businesses must ensure compliance with local and international regulations, particularly for restricted or controlled goods.

Shipping reliability is another crucial aspect of importing. Unexpected delays or supply chain disruptions can affect customer satisfaction and increase operational costs. Businesses should have contingency plans in place for potential interruptions, such as alternative suppliers or adjusted inventory management strategies.

Understanding the supply chain from production to delivery helps prevent sourcing risks. Knowing each link in the supply chain allows businesses to identify inefficiencies, anticipate problems, and establish better supplier relationships.

Building a Strong and Sustainable Supply Chain

Effective sourcing strategies combine cost efficiency, ethical responsibility, and supply chain stability. Businesses that evaluate suppliers carefully and prioritize sustainability can create a reliable, ethical, and competitive supply chain.

By assessing key factors such as cost, quality, sustainability, and lead times, businesses can make informed sourcing decisions that support long-term growth and align with company values. Whether sourcing locally, nationally, or internationally, a strategic approach to procurement ensures efficiency, profitability, and customer trust.

CHAPTER XVIII

Outsourcing Tasks

The Power of Outsourcing

Outsourcing operational tasks allows businesses to improve efficiency, reduce costs, and gain access to specialized expertise. While it requires investment, outsourcing enables companies to streamline processes, enhance service quality, and focus on core growth strategies. Understanding which areas to outsource and selecting the right partners can make a significant difference in business operations.

Key Areas Where Outsourcing Brings Value

Outsourcing is beneficial across multiple business functions, from marketing and IT support to manufacturing and financial management. Each area requires expertise, and external professionals can deliver high-quality results while allowing businesses to focus on strategic priorities.

Marketing and Brand Visibility

A strong marketing strategy is essential for customer engagement and brand recognition. Outsourcing various marketing functions can improve content quality, online presence, and lead generation efforts.

Professional content creators ensure that website articles, blogs, and promotional materials are compelling and aligned with brand messaging. Social media management services help maintain consistent engagement, strategic content planning, and real-time customer interactions. Email marketing specialists develop effective campaigns that increase conversions through audience segmentation and targeted messaging.

Website design and maintenance are also crucial for a strong digital presence. Regular updates, responsive design, and security measures contribute to a seamless user experience, which outsourced IT experts can handle efficiently. Additionally, search engine optimization (SEO) specialists ensure businesses rank higher in search engine results, boosting organic traffic and online visibility.

IT and Technological Integration

Businesses rely on technology to manage operations, connect with customers, and streamline internal processes. Outsourcing IT functions provides technical support, troubleshooting, and expert guidance on implementing essential systems.

Professional app developers can create custom applications that enhance customer engagement and business functionality. Businesses also benefit from experts who can integrate customer relationship management (CRM) and enterprise resource planning (ERP) systems, optimizing workflows and improving data analysis.

Customer Service and Logistics

Providing excellent customer support is essential for retaining clients and building loyalty. Outsourcing customer interactions ensures that inquiries, complaints, and after-sales service are handled professionally. Experienced agents can manage customer calls, emails, and chat support, improving response times and overall satisfaction.

Handling sales transactions and complaint resolution through third-party services ensures that customers receive quick and efficient assistance, preventing issues from escalating. Businesses can also invest in customer service training programs, equipping in-house teams with the skills to manage various scenarios effectively.

Logistics and inventory management can be complex, but third-party providers offer expertise in packaging, shipping, and supply chain optimization. By outsourcing these tasks, businesses can reduce overhead costs, improve delivery efficiency, and ensure timely order fulfillment.

Manufacturing and Production

Small businesses often lack the infrastructure needed for large-scale production. Outsourcing product manufacturing, design, and assembly enables businesses to create high-quality goods without major capital investments.

Professional manufacturers help with bulk production, prototype development, and component assembly, ensuring scalability as business demand grows. Additionally, expert product designers transform ideas into market-ready models, refining details for improved functionality and appeal.

Financial Management and Compliance

Handling payroll, accounting, and tax management requires precision and compliance with legal regulations. Outsourcing these functions to professional firms helps businesses avoid financial errors, maintain accurate records, and ensure timely payments.

Payroll services ensure employees receive accurate salaries, tax deductions, and benefits administration, reducing administrative burden. Accounting professionals manage financial reporting, tax preparation, and compliance, ensuring that businesses remain financially sound and legally compliant.

Sales tax management is another critical aspect, with experts handling tax calculations, submissions, and reporting to minimize the risk of errors and penalties.

Legal and Human Resource Support

Legal and HR requirements can be complex, making outsourcing a strategic choice for businesses looking to navigate contracts, compliance, and workforce management.

Legal advisors assist with drafting agreements, ensuring regulatory adherence, and resolving disputes, providing businesses with protection and legal security. HR specialists help with employee management, labor laws, and workforce planning, ensuring that policies align with industry best practices.

Outsourcing recruitment services saves time and effort by allowing experts to source, screen, and shortlist candidates who match business needs. This streamlines the hiring process and ensures that only qualified professionals are considered.

Why Businesses Should Consider Outsourcing

The advantages of outsourcing extend beyond just reducing workload. It provides businesses with access to high-level expertise, time efficiency, and scalability while ensuring focus remains on core growth areas.

- Cost Savings: Reduces operational expenses by eliminating the need for full-time staff in non-core areas.
- Specialized Expertise: Leverages professionals with industry knowledge, ensuring high-quality results.
- Time Efficiency: Allows businesses to dedicate more time to innovation and strategy rather than administrative tasks.
- Scalability: Makes it easier to expand or scale down operations without long-term commitments.
- Improved Focus: Keeps business owners and leadership teams focused on their key strengths while experts handle specific functions.

Building a Strong Business with Outsourcing

Outsourcing is a valuable strategy for businesses aiming to streamline operations, reduce costs, and enhance service quality. By identifying non-core tasks and collaborating with skilled service providers, businesses can optimize their efficiency and focus on growth and sustainability.

Strategic outsourcing allows businesses to operate smarter, compete effectively, and scale efficiently, ensuring long-term success in an evolving market.

CHAPTER XIX

Defining Your Brand

Laying the Foundation: Evaluating Your Business and Defining Your Brand

Before outsourcing or finalizing business strategies, it's essential to take a step back and evaluate the core functions of your business. Identifying areas where external support can add value ensures that resources are allocated efficiently. Whether you seek professional help, leverage personal networks, or use small business services, the key is to align your business needs with the right support systems.

A well-structured business operates with clear inventory management, logistics, service level agreements (SLAs), and warehousing. Inventory includes goods in production or ready for sale, while logistics covers the movement of these products to customers, ensuring smooth distribution and transportation. SLAs define the scope and expectations of outsourced services, while warehousing ensures proper storage before products reach retailers or consumers. These foundational elements play a crucial role in business efficiency, customer satisfaction, and operational success.

Choosing the Right Business Name

A business name is more than just a label—it is the cornerstone of your brand. It should be simple, memorable, and reflective of your company's values and offerings. While creativity is important, a name that is too complex, ambiguous, or overly humorous may not translate well to a broad audience. The best names have clarity, uniqueness, and a strong connection to the business purpose.

To ensure your chosen name stands out, consider using alliteration, creative word combinations, or personal and location-based elements. Checking business registers, trademark databases, domain availability, and social media ensures that the name is legally viable and avoids confusion with existing brands.

Once selected, the name should be registered with government agencies and local authorities, securing trademarks and digital assets, including a website domain. If forming an LLC or Inc., it is important to include the appropriate suffix to maintain legal compliance.

Crafting a Strong and Authentic Brand

Branding extends beyond a logo or tagline; it is the essence of how your business is perceived. A well-developed brand builds trust, loyalty, and a strong emotional connection with customers. It should reflect the company's values, maintain consistency across all platforms, and reinforce authenticity through actions that align with its messaging.

A business must define its purpose and clearly articulate the benefits of its products or services. Whether positioning itself as bold and innovative, traditional and reliable, or approachable and customer-centric, brand personality should resonate with the target audience. This identity is communicated through design, marketing, and direct customer interactions.

A brand's effectiveness depends on consistent messaging across multiple channels. Engaging visuals, memorable slogans, and a well-maintained online presence reinforce brand recognition. Social media, websites, and email marketing play crucial roles in connecting with customers and maintaining engagement.

Building Lasting Customer Relationships

Branding isn't just about recognition—it's about forming long-term connections with customers. Trust and loyalty come from repeated positive experiences, transparency, and delivering on promises. Businesses that stay true to their core values create repeat customers and strong brand advocates.

One of the most powerful ways to establish an emotional connection is through storytelling. A compelling brand story should go beyond business transactions and focus on the motivation behind the business, lessons learned, current impact, and vision for the future. This narrative differentiates a brand from competitors, fosters trust, and attracts both loyal and new customers.

Crafting a Meaningful Brand Story

A strong brand story answers key questions about the business's origin and evolution. Understanding the motivation behind the business provides authenticity, while insights gained along the journey shape its purpose. Current operations should align with customer expectations, and the long-term vision should reflect aspirations for growth and innovation.

A successful brand story also connects with the emotions of the audience. Identifying customer needs, desires, and values allows businesses to tailor messaging in a way that resonates. Shared values create a sense of belonging, encouraging customers to form deeper relationships with the brand.

Spreading the Word and Adapting Over Time

Once the brand story is established, it should be communicated consistently across various platforms. Social media plays a crucial role in sharing narratives through visuals, videos, and direct engagement with followers. A well-structured website should include compelling stories and customer testimonials to reinforce credibility. Collaborations with influencers or industry experts help amplify brand reach and build trust within specific communities.

As businesses grow, branding should evolve to remain relevant. Regularly revisiting and refining the brand's story ensures that it continues to reflect the company's progress and customer expectations. Authenticity is key—businesses that overpromise or present a misleading image risk damaging their reputation. A unique, well-crafted narrative that aligns with business operations strengthens customer loyalty and long-term success.

Avoiding Common Branding Pitfalls

Brand credibility is built on honesty, uniqueness, and consistency. Making false claims or exaggerating achievements can erode trust and damage a company's reputation. A generic or uninspired brand story may fail to engage customers, while a disconnect between brand messaging and actual business practices can create skepticism. To maintain authenticity, internal teams should be well-versed in the brand's mission and values, ensuring alignment in every aspect of the business.

Creating a Lasting Impact Through Branding

Thoughtfully crafting a brand and sharing its story allows businesses to establish a distinctive identity in the marketplace. A strong brand is more than a marketing tool—it is the foundation of trust, customer loyalty, and long-term business growth. By staying true to core values, communicating effectively, and fostering meaningful connections, businesses create a memorable presence that stands the test of time.

CHAPTER XX

A Blend of Marketing

Blending the 4Ps and 4Cs: A Balanced Approach to Marketing Success

Marketing is the bridge between a business and its customers, and an effective strategy requires both a business-driven approach and a customer-centric perspective. The 4Ps framework—Product, Price, Promotion, and Place—focuses on business-led decisions, shaping how a company presents its offerings to the market. Meanwhile, the 4Cs framework—Commodity, Cost, Communication, and Convenience—prioritizes customer needs and expectations, ensuring a strong connection with the target audience. By integrating these two models, businesses can develop a well-rounded marketing strategy that achieves both business growth and customer satisfaction.

The 4Ps: A Business-Centered Approach

The 4Ps framework provides businesses with a structured way to develop and position their products in the market. Each element plays a role in ensuring a product reaches the right audience with the right message.

Product: Creating the Right Offering

A product's success depends on its design, features, and overall appeal to customers. It should not only serve a functional purpose but also align with customer preferences and expectations. Identifying what makes a product unique—whether through superior quality, innovation, or exclusive benefits—creates differentiation from competitors. Businesses must also evaluate how their product stacks up against others in terms of performance, durability, and overall user experience.

Price: Finding the Right Balance

Pricing is more than just setting a number—it influences customer perception and directly impacts sales. Market research helps determine industry standards and competitor pricing, but businesses must also consider customer willingness to pay and perceived value. Small adjustments in pricing can have a significant effect on profitability, and testing different price points helps identify the optimal balance between affordability and business sustainability.

Promotion: Reaching the Right Audience

A well-planned promotion strategy ensures that the right audience receives the right message at the right time. Businesses must choose effective communication channels—whether through social media, print advertising, or digital campaigns—to maximize reach. Understanding customer preferences helps tailor promotions, such as discounts, free samples, or limited-time offers, to increase engagement. Timing is also crucial, as seasonal trends and customer behavior patterns influence responsiveness to marketing campaigns.

Place: Ensuring Accessibility and Availability

A great product must be available where customers prefer to shop, whether online, in physical stores, or through direct sales. Businesses must study customer shopping habits to optimize distribution channels and ensure easy access to their products. A streamlined supply chain improves efficiency, reduces costs, and ensures timely delivery, making a product more attractive to potential buyers.

The 4Cs: A Customer-Focused Approach

While the 4Ps focus on how a business positions and markets its products, the 4Cs emphasize the customer's experience and expectations. This framework helps businesses ensure their offerings truly meet customer needs.

Commodity: Understanding Customer Expectations

From a customer's perspective, a product is not just an item but a solution to a specific need or problem. Instead of focusing solely on product features, businesses must consider what value and benefits the product provides. Aligning product design with customer expectations improves satisfaction and increases brand loyalty.

Cost: The Customer's Perspective on Pricing

While businesses determine price points based on profitability, customers focus on the overall cost-to-value ratio. Some consumers prioritize affordability, while others are willing to pay more for premium quality or added convenience. Businesses must ensure that pricing reflects the perceived value of the product, making customers feel they are making a worthwhile investment.

Communication: Engaging and Informing Customers

Traditional promotion focuses on spreading awareness, but communication involves two-way engagement with customers. Businesses must craft messages that resonate both emotionally and practically, addressing pain points and highlighting benefits. Understanding where customers seek information—whether through social media, emails, or traditional advertising—allows businesses to communicate effectively and build long-term relationships rather than just transactional interactions.

Convenience: Simplifying the Customer Journey

Customers prioritize convenience, and businesses must ensure that their buying journey is as seamless as possible. This means making products available through multiple channels, offering simple checkout processes, and minimizing barriers to purchase. The easier it is for customers to access, evaluate, and buy a product, the higher the chances of conversion and repeat business.

Integrating the 4Ps and 4Cs for a Holistic Marketing Strategy

Rather than choosing between the 4Ps or 4Cs, businesses should combine both models to create a marketing approach that balances business goals with customer expectations.

- Product vs. Commodity: Instead of just listing product features, businesses should focus on how their offerings solve problems or improve customers' lives.
- Price vs. Cost: Pricing should not only be competitive but also justify the value customers receive, ensuring affordability without compromising quality.
- Promotion vs. Communication: Beyond just advertising, businesses should engage in meaningful interactions with customers, creating trust and long-term relationships.
- Place vs. Convenience: Distribution strategies should align with how customers prefer to shop, ensuring accessibility and a smooth purchasing experience.

Achieving Long-Term Success Through Customer-Centric Marketing

By blending the business-driven 4Ps with the customer-oriented 4Cs, businesses can create effective marketing strategies that attract, engage, and retain customers. This approach ensures that offerings are not only competitive in the market but also resonate deeply with the target audience, leading to increased sales, stronger brand loyalty, and sustainable business growth.

CHAPTER XXI

The Sales Procedure

The Sales Process: Building Relationships and Driving Growth

Even with high-quality products or services, success in business depends on effective selling. The sales process goes beyond completing transactions—it's about establishing trust, offering value, and nurturing customer loyalty. A strong sales strategy ensures repeat business and generates referrals, driving long-term growth.

Building Customer Relationships

Successful sales begin with trust. Engaging with customers regularly, answering questions promptly, and addressing concerns create a reliable and credible brand presence. Personalized communication plays a crucial role, as customers respond better when solutions are tailored to their unique needs. Speaking their language—both in terms of tone and content—ensures a stronger connection. Ongoing support, including after-sales service and follow-ups, enhances customer experience, reinforcing satisfaction and brand loyalty.

The Sales Funnel: Converting Prospects into Customers

The sales funnel represents the customer journey from initial awareness to making a purchase. Each stage requires a different approach to guide prospects toward a successful transaction.

Awareness: Capturing Attention

At this stage, potential customers first learn about your product or service. To build brand visibility, businesses must use multiple promotional strategies. Content marketing through blogs and articles helps address customer concerns while positioning the business as an industry authority. Social media engagement fosters direct interactions, while targeted advertising boosts brand recognition through online or traditional media. Well-placed product displays in high-traffic areas—both online and offline—ensure exposure to potential buyers. The goal is to stand out from competitors and remain top-of-mind for consumers.

Interest: Generating Engagement

Once customers are aware of the brand, the next step is to develop interest. This is achieved by highlighting how the product or service solves specific problems. Case studies, whitepapers, or detailed product descriptions provide valuable insights into its benefits. Storytelling plays a powerful role in sales—connecting emotionally with an audience through real-life examples strengthens engagement and trust. By consistently demonstrating value, businesses move prospects closer to making a decision.

Decision: Overcoming Objections

At this stage, potential buyers compare options and evaluate their choices. Businesses can facilitate the decision-making process by offering customer testimonials and positive reviews to establish credibility. Product comparisons help customers understand the advantages over competing alternatives. Promotional incentives, such as discounts or exclusive offers, can encourage them to act. A clear call to action, whether through a seamless checkout process or a well-timed sales prompt, removes hesitation and guides customers toward the final step.

Action: Completing the Sale

The last stage is where the customer finalizes the purchase. Ensuring that the checkout process is straightforward and friction-free improves conversion rates. Offering multiple payment options accommodates different customer preferences. Post-purchase engagement, such as confirmation messages, thank-you notes, or product usage tips, reinforces trust and encourages future interactions. Businesses that provide an easy, positive buying experience increase customer satisfaction and the likelihood of repeat sales.

Choosing the Right Sales Channels

The success of a product depends not only on how it's marketed but also on where it's sold. Identifying the best sales channels requires analyzing customer buying behavior, product characteristics, and audience preferences. Some customers prefer online shopping, while others rely on in-store experiences. Aligning sales efforts with how customers prefer to shop ensures accessibility and convenience.

Order Fulfillment and Customer Satisfaction

Making a sale is only the beginning. Ensuring prompt and efficient order fulfillment builds customer trust and encourages repeat business. Streamlining delivery processes minimizes errors and improves efficiency. As demand grows, businesses may consider outsourcing fulfillment to third-party providers, allowing for scalability without compromising service quality.

Maintaining Customer Retention and Pricing Strategies

Retaining existing customers is often more cost-effective than acquiring new ones. Customers who have already made purchases are the best prospects for future sales. Understanding what they value most—whether it's competitive pricing, quality service, or personalized offers—enables businesses to adjust their pricing and communication strategies accordingly.

Actively listening to customer feedback provides valuable insights into improvements and helps refine the sales approach. Businesses that remain responsive and adaptable cultivate stronger relationships, increasing brand loyalty and long-term profitability.

Optimizing Sales for Growth and Success

A strong sales process goes beyond closing deals—it builds long-lasting customer relationships and drives sustainable business growth. By focusing on customer needs, using the right sales channels, and refining fulfillment strategies, businesses can create a seamless, engaging experience that boosts loyalty and maximizes revenue. Effective selling is not just about transactions—it's about delivering value, earning trust, and ensuring that customers keep coming back.

CHAPTER XXII

E-commerce

E-Commerce: Expanding Business Opportunities in the Digital Age

E-commerce has transformed the way businesses operate, allowing them to reach a broader audience with lower operational costs. Selling online eliminates the need for physical storefronts and provides opportunities for rapid growth. Choosing the right e-commerce platform is crucial, as each option has its own benefits and challenges.

Choosing the Right E-Commerce Method

Businesses can sell online through custom websites, site builders, or established marketplaces, depending on their goals, budget, and expertise.

A dedicated website offers full control over branding, design, and customer interactions. It allows businesses to build a unique identity, optimize SEO, and operate independently of third-party algorithms. However, it requires investment in development, security, and maintenance, making it a more complex and costly option.

For those seeking an easier setup, e-commerce site builders like Shopify, Wix, or Squarespace provide user-friendly tools, security management, and affordability. While they simplify operations, customization is limited, and businesses must pay subscription fees.

Selling through online marketplaces like Amazon, eBay, or Etsy offers immediate access to a large customer base with built-in logistics and marketing support. However, these platforms come with high competition, commission fees, and restricted control over branding.

Maximizing Online Success

Operating an online business goes beyond setting up a store. Visibility and customer engagement are key to standing out in a competitive digital marketplace.

For businesses running their own websites, search engine optimization (SEO) helps attract organic traffic. Effective strategies include keyword optimization, informative content creation, and backlink building.

For those using third-party platforms, success depends on clear product descriptions, high-quality images, competitive pricing, and adherence to marketplace policies.

Efficient order fulfillment is also crucial. Meeting delivery expectations builds trust and encourages repeat purchases. As businesses scale, outsourcing fulfillment to third-party providers can enhance efficiency and customer satisfaction.

Navigating the Future of E-Commerce

E-commerce offers businesses the flexibility to sell globally, operate 24/7, and scale efficiently. Choosing the right platform depends on business goals, technical expertise, and market strategy. Whether building a website, using a site builder, or leveraging online marketplaces, understanding each method's strengths and challenges ensures long-term success in the digital marketplace.

CHAPTER XXIII

Offering a Service

Providing Exceptional Services: Building Trust and Long-Term Success

Unlike selling products, offering a service is deeply rooted in trust and perceived value. Clients evaluate services based on experience, making every interaction an opportunity to strengthen relationships and ensure repeat business. Success in a service-based business depends on credibility, consistency, and customer-centricity.

Building and Maintaining Trust

Trust is the foundation of any service. Clients must believe in your expertise and reliability, as they can't assess a service before purchasing. Being transparent about capabilities and limitations reinforces credibility. If a particular request is outside your expertise, recommending a trusted alternative builds goodwill. Consistency in delivering high-quality service strengthens this trust over time, ensuring clients return.

Evolving Through Client Feedback

Every interaction is a chance to refine and improve. Actively gathering client feedback helps identify areas for growth and innovation. Businesses that listen, adapt, and evolve remain relevant and competitive. Understanding market trends and client expectations allows for adjustments that enhance service quality. Flexibility ensures that services continue to meet changing demands.

Fostering Client Loyalty

Long-term success is built on client loyalty. Delivering consistently high-quality service ensures satisfaction, while adding a personal touch makes clients feel valued. Recognizing preferences, remembering key milestones, and offering incentives like loyalty rewards or exclusive perks strengthen relationships. Clients who feel appreciated are more likely to return and recommend your services.

Understanding and Exceeding Expectations

Success lies in anticipating and surpassing client expectations. Effective communication is key—regular check-ins help ensure services align with their evolving needs. A proactive approach, personalized attention, and taking responsibility for any issues reinforce professionalism. Unexpected acts of appreciation, such as a thank-you note or a complimentary service, leave a lasting impression.

Simplifying the Client Experience

Clients appreciate a smooth, hassle-free experience. Making services easy to access, providing quick responses to inquiries, and streamlining processes like booking and payment enhance customer satisfaction. A professional, yet friendly approach encourages open communication and stronger relationships.

Ensuring Reliable Service Delivery

Trust is earned by consistently delivering on promises. A well-structured Service Level Agreement (SLA) helps manage expectations by outlining service quality, responsibilities, and timelines. Periodic evaluations ensure services remain efficient, effective, and competitive. Addressing issues promptly reinforces commitment to customer satisfaction.

Sustaining Growth and Innovation

A thriving service business requires continuous learning and adaptation. Keeping in touch with clients through valuable updates and newsletters, staying informed about competitors, and regularly improving service offerings are essential for long-term success. Addressing concerns immediately maintains credibility, while exploring complementary services broadens revenue opportunities.

Creating Meaningful Client Relationships

At the heart of every successful service business is a strong, trust-based relationship with clients. By being honest, proactive, and customer-focused, businesses create lasting loyalty. Every interaction should be treated as an opportunity to strengthen connections, ensuring that clients return and refer others. Trust, once established, becomes the foundation for sustainable success.

CHAPTER XXIV

Processing Payments

Efficient Payment Processing: Enhancing Transactions and Customer Trust

Smooth payment processing is essential for any business, ensuring secure, convenient, and seamless transactions. Offering multiple payment options—both electronic and offline—improves customer satisfaction and reduces the risk of lost sales. A well-integrated payment system streamlines operations, enhances security, and ensures a steady cash flow.

Understanding the Payment Process Flow

Every transaction follows a structured process, ensuring payments are securely verified and transferred.

1. Customer Provides Payment Information

    - In-person payments involve credit/debit cards or mobile wallets like Google Pay and Apple Pay at a payment terminal.
    - Online transactions require customers to enter card or digital wallet details on a website or app.

2. Authorization Request Sent

- The payment processor collects transaction details and securely transmits them to the customer's bank for approval.

3. Transaction Approval or Decline

- The customer's bank verifies funds and credentials. If valid, the payment is approved; otherwise, it's declined.

4. Settlement and Fund Transfer

- Approved transactions are sent for settlement, where multiple transactions may be batched before transferring funds to the merchant's account.

Electronic Payment Systems

Businesses typically partner with merchant service providers to accept digital payments, integrating both payment gateways (online) and payment processors (in-person). These systems connect the customer's bank with the merchant's bank, ensuring secure and efficient transactions.

Merchant accounts help businesses process payments, handle refunds, and prevent fraud. E-payment systems enable cashless transactions, including credit/debit cards and mobile wallets.

Offline Payment Alternatives

For customers who prefer traditional payment methods, offering offline options ensures accessibility and convenience.

- Bank Deposits & Wire Transfers: Secure, direct transactions where funds are transferred from the customer's bank to the business account.
- Checks & Money Orders: Physical payments that require clearance before processing an order.
- Cross-Border Payment Platforms: Facilitate international transactions efficiently.

Key Terms in Payment Processing

- Acquiring Bank: The merchant's bank that receives funds from the customer's bank.
- Digital Wallet: Secure software for storing payment details (e.g., PayPal, Google Pay).
- POS System: Software for processing payments and managing inventory.
- Payment Services Provider (PSP): A combined payment gateway and merchant service solution.

Optimizing Payment Systems for Business Growth

To maximize efficiency, businesses should offer multiple payment options, ensure security with trusted gateways, and streamline the checkout experience. Staying updated on emerging payment technologies helps maintain a competitive edge and improves customer satisfaction. Implementing a reliable and secure payment infrastructure builds trust, enhances user experience, and ensures smooth financial transactions, contributing to long-term success.

CHAPTER XXV

Completing Orders

Optimizing Order Fulfillment for Customer Satisfaction and Growth

For businesses selling and delivering products, an efficient order fulfillment system is essential for maintaining customer trust and ensuring smooth operations. A well-structured process minimizes errors, speeds up delivery, and strengthens brand loyalty, ultimately driving repeat business and long-term success.

The Order Fulfillment Process

A smooth fulfillment system ensures that every step—from order placement to delivery—is handled efficiently.

Processing Orders and Confirmations

Once an order is placed, verifying product availability is the first step. Customers should receive an immediate confirmation with their order details and estimated delivery time. Keeping customers informed builds trust and sets clear expectations.

Stock Management and Product Preparation

Depending on the business model, products may be either manufactured on demand or retrieved from inventory.

Accurate real-time inventory tracking prevents stockouts and overselling. Proper packaging enhances product safety and creates a positive unboxing experience, reinforcing brand professionalism.

Shipping and Distribution

Choosing the right delivery method is crucial for timely service. Local deliveries may benefit from direct dispatching, while long-distance shipments require reliable courier partnerships. High-value items should be insured to protect against damage or loss. Providing tracking details and delivery updates reassures customers and reduces inquiries about order status.

Handling Returns and Customer Support

A transparent return and exchange policy ensures customer confidence. Including return instructions in order confirmations simplifies the process and improves overall satisfaction.

Meeting Customer Expectations

As online shopping continues to grow, consumers expect fast delivery and hassle-free returns. Ensuring sufficient stock availability and maintaining accurate inventory records streamline order processing. Businesses can start with manual tracking but should transition to fulfillment software as demand scales.

For larger operations, outsourcing fulfillment to third-party logistics (3PL) providers can help maintain service quality and efficiency. Choosing the right fulfillment partner ensures that delivery speed, packaging, and customer service align with brand expectations.

Managing Costs and Budgeting for Fulfillment

Starting and scaling a fulfillment system requires careful budgeting. Businesses must assess initial expenses, including inventory, warehousing, and software, while balancing immediate needs with long-term investments.

Cost Management Strategies

To reduce expenses, businesses can consider:

- Leasing equipment instead of purchasing to lower upfront costs.
- Using refurbished assets for sustainability and affordability.
- Sharing storage or logistics resources with other businesses to minimize overhead.

Buying vs. Leasing Assets

Owning fulfillment assets provides long-term savings but requires higher upfront investment. Leasing offers greater flexibility, making it ideal for businesses in early stages or experiencing fluctuating demand.

Building an Efficient Fulfillment System

Starting small with spreadsheets or manual tracking is an affordable approach, but as demand grows, automating fulfillment processes becomes essential. Businesses should focus on delivering consistently on time, refining logistics, and adapting systems as sales increase.

A well-optimized fulfillment strategy enhances customer experience, strengthens trust, and encourages repeat purchases, positioning a business for long-term success.

CHAPTER XXVI

Determining Initial Expenses

Managing Startup Costs: Smart Planning for a Strong Business Launch

Starting a business requires balancing essential expenses with available funds, ensuring that initial investments are strategic and cost-effective. By prioritizing key needs and exploring affordable alternatives, businesses can establish a solid foundation without unnecessary financial strain.

Essential Startup Costs and How to Manage Them

Premises Setup

For businesses requiring a physical space, upfront payments like rent, security deposits, and advance payments must be accounted for. Renovations or customizations may be needed to create a welcoming or professional environment. Ensuring compliance with health and safety regulations is crucial, requiring inspections and certifications before opening.

Utilities and Operational Costs

Setting up electricity, water, internet, and telecom services is essential. Businesses can reduce ongoing costs by choosing discounted business packages from service providers.

Legal and Compliance Expenses

Businesses must secure the necessary permits, licenses, and insurance based on their industry and location. Consulting a professional helps navigate legal requirements, reducing the risk of compliance issues.

Equipment and Technology

Investing in essential tools, machinery, and IT systems ensures smooth operations. Instead of purchasing everything upfront, businesses can lease, rent, or buy refurbished equipment to save costs. Reliable computers, point-of-sale systems, and accounting software are also crucial for managing business functions efficiently.

Inventory Management

Stocking up on raw materials or finished products should be based on realistic sales forecasts to avoid overstocking and unnecessary storage costs. Businesses should adjust stock levels gradually based on demand trends.

Marketing and Branding

Creating a strong brand identity, including a professional logo and cohesive messaging, helps establish credibility. A well-planned launch strategy incorporating digital ads, social media campaigns, and promotional materials maximizes visibility.

Website and Online Presence

An effective online presence starts with securing a domain name, hosting, and a user-friendly website. Affordable website builders or professional designers can create a site that enhances credibility. Cybersecurity measures, such as SSL certificates and malware protection, safeguard customer data.

Smart Budgeting Strategies

- Leasing and renting expensive equipment instead of purchasing upfront.
- Buying refurbished tools and IT products to reduce expenses without compromising quality.
- Exploring grants or startup loans that provide financial assistance for new businesses.

By strategically managing expenses and seeking cost-effective solutions, businesses can launch efficiently while maintaining financial flexibility. Careful planning ensures a strong start, reduced financial pressure, and long-term sustainability.

CHAPTER XXVII

Budget

Planning Your Business Budget: Smart Financial Management for a Strong Start

Launching a business requires careful financial planning to cover essential costs while avoiding unnecessary spending. Accurately estimating expenses ensures financial stability and helps secure funding. A well-structured budget includes one-time startup costs, ongoing operational expenses, and essential assets to keep the business running smoothly.

Identifying and Categorizing Expenses

Business costs can be divided into three main categories: business assets, one-off setup costs, and recurring expenses.

Business Assets: These are long-term investments that provide value over time. This includes inventory, IT equipment, office furniture, and vehicles for transportation or deliveries. Investing wisely in these assets ensures smooth operations while managing initial expenditures.

One-Time Setup Costs: These expenses are incurred before the business officially starts and often include branding, website development, legal fees, marketing, and premises setup. While many of these are tax-deductible, they should be prioritized based on their impact on the business's launch and reputation.

Ongoing Operational Expenses: Monthly and yearly costs such as utilities, payroll, IT maintenance, raw materials, advertising, and loan repayments are crucial for sustaining business growth. Budgeting for these ensures steady cash flow and financial stability.

Prioritizing Expenses and Cost-Saving Strategies

Startups should focus on essential items first, investing in branding, website setup, and legal compliance to establish credibility. Cost-saving measures such as leasing equipment, buying refurbished technology, and using affordable software solutions can significantly reduce initial expenditures.

For businesses working with limited resources, minimizing expenses while maintaining efficiency is key. This includes upgrading existing computers instead of buying new ones, sourcing second-hand office furniture, and leveraging free or low-cost marketing tools like social media. Hiring freelancers or contract workers for specialized tasks rather than full-time employees can also reduce costs in the early stages.

Estimating and Managing Startup Costs

A structured approach to budgeting ensures that all necessary expenses are covered. Creating a detailed spreadsheet listing business assets, initial costs, and recurring expenses helps track expenditures and maintain financial control.

Assessing financial health by comparing projected expenses with expected revenue helps businesses plan for high-cost periods, estimate their break-even point, and set realistic financial goals. By adopting a strategic, cost-effective approach, startups can maintain financial stability while positioning themselves for long-term success.

CHAPTER XXVIII

Earning Target

Setting an Earning Target: Balancing Business and Personal Finances

To achieve financial stability as a business owner, it's essential to calculate both business and personal expenses. This ensures that your business generates enough revenue to cover operational costs, personal income, and future growth investments. Many new businesses experience low earnings in the initial stages, requiring careful financial planning to sustain operations and personal expenses.

Estimating Income and Business Viability

A business owner's income typically comes from salary and dividends, but the business must first generate enough revenue to sustain itself. Early on, profits are often reinvested into growth, meaning personal earnings may be minimal. Setting a realistic timeline for profitability helps determine when the business can start providing a stable income.

To assess business viability, estimate potential income over the first 6-12 months and subtract key expenses:

- Start-Up Costs (one-time expenses that must eventually be repaid)
- Running Costs (ongoing operational expenses)

- Investment & Contingency Funds (for growth and unforeseen expenses)

By comparing potential earnings against these expenses, you can evaluate whether your business will generate sufficient profits to cover both operational needs and your personal living costs.

Key Expenses to Consider

Start-Up Costs include premises setup, inventory, staffing, equipment, website development, legal fees, and marketing. These initial investments lay the foundation for business operations.

Running Costs cover utilities, raw materials, payroll, advertising, IT maintenance, and other recurring expenses necessary for daily operations. Keeping these manageable is essential for long-term sustainability.

Investment & Contingency Funds ensure financial stability, covering emergency expenses, product development, and market research to remain competitive.

Personal Financial Needs such as housing, utilities, daily expenses, loan repayments, entertainment, and savings must also be factored in. Your business should ideally generate enough income to support these costs over time.

Planning for Taxes and Future Growth

After estimating business income, tax obligations must be deducted to determine actual take-home earnings. Tracking business and personal expenses regularly ensures financial stability, preventing overspending.

While it may take time to earn a stable income, strategic reinvestment in growth, careful expense management, and realistic financial planning will position the business for long-term success. By setting clear earning targets, businesses can balance sustainability, profitability, and financial security.

CHAPTER XXIX

Financing Your Business

Securing Funding: Choosing the Right Financial Path for Your Business

Launching and sustaining a business requires adequate funding, and understanding the available options helps entrepreneurs make informed financial decisions. While bootstrapping—using personal savings—is ideal for businesses with low startup costs, many ventures require external funding to scale. Businesses can access funds through debt financing, crowdfunding, or equity financing, each with its own advantages and challenges.

Exploring Funding Options

Bootstrapping: This self-funded approach allows business owners to retain full control without debt. While effective for low-cost startups, it requires careful budgeting and resourcefulness. Businesses with minimal overhead—such as service-based or web-based companies—often benefit the most.

Debt Financing: Bank loans, business credit cards, or asset-backed financing provide quick capital without giving up ownership. While this approach helps manage cash flow and retain full profits, it comes with interest rates, repayment obligations, and potential collateral requirements. A strong business plan improves approval chances.

Equity Financing: Selling shares in exchange for capital provides access to significant funding without debt. Investors often bring industry expertise and valuable networks, accelerating business growth. However, this requires giving up partial control and sharing profits, making it a long-term commitment.

Choosing the Right Funding Strategy

The ideal funding route depends on several factors:

- Industry and Business Model: Bootstrapping works well for service-based businesses, while product-based companies often need debt or equity financing.
- Funding Requirements: Small-scale ventures may rely on personal savings or crowdfunding, whereas larger businesses may need investor backing or loans.
- Control and Flexibility: Entrepreneurs unwilling to share decision-making power may prefer debt financing over equity investment.

Meeting Financial Obligations

Regardless of the funding method, businesses must review all financial commitments carefully. Debt financing requires consistent repayments, making cash flow management essential. Equity financing involves aligning with investor expectations, often requiring structured growth plans. Consulting with an accountant ensures realistic financial projections and compliance.

Business credit cards offer additional flexibility, helping manage cash flow while tracking expenses separately.

However, eligibility depends on credit history, and high interest rates can pose risks if balances aren't paid on time.

Strategic Financial Planning for Growth

Choosing the right funding approach depends on business needs, risk tolerance, and long-term goals. Entrepreneurs should assess financial projections, ensure repayment capabilities, and align funding decisions with growth strategies. By securing the right financial resources, businesses can build a sustainable foundation for expansion and long-term success.

CHAPTER XXX

Investors

Choosing the Right Investors: Understanding Your Funding Options

Securing investment is a crucial step in growing a business, and selecting the right type of investor requires careful consideration. Different investors come with varying levels of control, repayment terms, and expectations, making it important to align funding choices with long-term business goals.

Types of Potential Investors

Family and Friends

Relying on personal connections can provide flexible repayment terms and emotional support, but it also carries the risk of straining relationships if the business struggles. Open and honest discussions about expectations and risks are essential before accepting financial support from loved ones.

Peer-to-Peer (P2P) Lending

Online lending platforms allow businesses to secure funding from individuals rather than banks. These platforms often offer lower interest rates, but they can affect credit ratings if repayments aren't met. P2P funding also depends on building trust and maintaining a strong reputation among investors.

Bank Loans

Traditional bank loans provide structured debt financing without equity loss, meaning business owners retain full control. However, banks often require strong credit ratings, collateral, and detailed financial projections, making it harder for startups to qualify.

Business Angels

Angel investors not only offer capital but also mentorship and business connections. They make quick investment decisions but often seek partial control or profit-sharing, making it crucial to assess how much influence you are willing to give up.

Venture Capitalists

Venture capitalists fund businesses with high growth potential and provide leadership, networking, and strategic collaboration. Unlike loans, there's no repayment obligation, but in exchange, venture capitalists take equity and decision-making influence. They expect rapid growth and high returns, and underperformance can lead to loss of control over the business.

Government Grants and Charities

Non-repayable grants from government programs, local authorities, or charities provide financial support without equity loss or repayment obligations. However, they often have strict conditions, competitive application processes, and funding restrictions on how the money can be used.

Selecting the Right Investor for Your Business

The ideal investor depends on factors like control, repayment terms, and mentorship opportunities. Business owners must determine whether they prefer maintaining full ownership (e.g., bootstrapping or bank loans) or are open to sharing equity for expertise and capital growth (e.g., angel investors or venture capitalists).

Understanding Funding Structures

Investors can support startups through either debt financing or equity investment. Debt financing, such as loans or credit lines, requires regular repayment with interest. Equity investment, in contrast, involves selling a share of the business in exchange for capital, allowing investors to influence decisions and share in future profits.

Choosing the right funding method ensures that financial decisions align with business stability, long-term growth, and operational flexibility. A well-informed approach to investment can fuel expansion while maintaining financial security.

CHAPTER XXXI

Accelerators and Incubators

Accelerators and Incubators: Boosting Your Startup's Growth

Launching a startup can be challenging, but accelerators and incubators provide valuable support, funding, and mentorship to help businesses scale successfully. Understanding the differences between these programs will help you choose the right one for your business needs.

Accelerators: Fast-Tracking Business Growth

Accelerators are short-term, intensive programs designed to help startups scale quickly, typically lasting three to six months. These programs focus on rapid growth, mentorship, and securing investment opportunities.

Key Benefits of Accelerators

- Mentorship: Guidance from experienced entrepreneurs and industry experts.
- Seed Funding: Many accelerators offer initial capital to help startups grow.
- Networking: Access to investors, partners, and other startups.
- Growth Focus: Programs are designed to help businesses launch or secure investment quickly.

What Accelerators Expect in Return

- Equity Stake: Typically, accelerators take 5% to 10% ownership in exchange for funding and support.
- Full Commitment: Participants must be fully involved for the program's duration.
- Performance Milestones: Startups are expected to show measurable progress.

Incubators: Nurturing Long-Term Success

Unlike accelerators, incubators provide longer-term support, often lasting one to five years. They help startups refine their business models, develop products, and prepare for scaling. Many incubators are backed by universities, nonprofits, or government programs.

Key Benefits of Incubators

- Extended Mentorship: Ongoing guidance to refine business operations.
- Affordable Office Space: Many incubators offer shared workspaces, reducing operational costs.
- Networking: Opportunities to connect with industry professionals, investors, and fellow entrepreneurs.
- Access to Specialized Facilities: Tech-focused incubators may provide labs or advanced equipment.

What Incubators Expect in Return

- Equity Stake or Subsidized Rent: Some incubators take a small equity share (5-10%), while others charge a subsidized rent for workspace.
- Commitment to Growth: Startups are expected to continuously develop their business models.

Choosing Between an Accelerator and an Incubator

Accelerators are ideal for startups ready to scale quickly and seek investment within a short period. They work best for businesses with a solid product and clear growth potential.

Incubators are better suited for early-stage startups that need time to develop their business model, test ideas, and refine operations before seeking investors.

Industries That Benefit Most from Incubators

- Tech Startups: Software, hardware, and engineering businesses gain access to tech-specific resources.
- Healthcare & Biotech: Science-based businesses benefit from specialized lab spaces and research facilities.
- Social Enterprises: Nonprofits and sustainability-driven startups can find mission-aligned incubators.

Maximizing Startup Success

Both accelerators and incubators offer valuable mentorship, funding, and networking. Startups should carefully evaluate their growth stage, financial needs, and long-term goals before choosing the right program. Whether you need rapid scaling or long-term development, these programs provide critical support to help your business thrive.

CHAPTER XXXII

Presenting for Investment

Mastering the Investor Pitch: Presenting Your Startup with Confidence

Securing funding requires more than just a great idea—it demands a compelling pitch that demonstrates business viability, market potential, and scalability. Investors look for clarity, enthusiasm, and realistic financial planning. A well-structured pitch balances storytelling, data, and a clear ask for funding.

Preparing to Pitch

Before approaching investors, research their interests and past investments to tailor your presentation accordingly. Begin with a concise elevator pitch that clearly defines what your business offers and why it matters. Follow this by detailing the problem your business solves, your unique solution, and market potential, using visuals to reinforce key points. Clearly state how much funding you need and how it will be used. Practicing beforehand ensures you deliver with confidence and clarity.

Online Presentations: Navigating Virtual Pitches

When pitching via platforms like Zoom or Google Meet, technical preparation is crucial. Test your internet connection, ensure your slides are clear, and anticipate possible issues. Virtual settings demand a more direct approach—keep your message engaging and to the point, while allowing room for questions and discussion. Be mindful of delays and interruptions.

Delivering a Persuasive Pitch

1. Clearly Define Your Business and Value Proposition

- Explain what your business offers in a simple and compelling way.
- Demonstrate how your product or service solves a real problem and why customers will choose it.
- Highlight what makes your business unique compared to competitors.

2. Show Market Demand and Scalability

- Define your target audience and why they will buy.
- Use data and market research to prove demand and customer interest.
- Outline a scaling strategy to assure investors of long-term growth.

3. Address Competition and Your Advantage

- Show awareness of existing competitors and how you differentiate.
- Emphasize your competitive edge, whether through pricing, technology, or customer experience.

Engaging Investors and Avoiding Pitfalls

A strong pitch is clear, concise, and engaging. Keep it short and focused, encourage questions, and support claims with data. Investors value enthusiasm, but your projections must be realistic—overpromising weakens credibility. Avoid technical jargon, excessive details, and reading from slides. Use visuals effectively, maintain confidence, and conclude with a clear call to action, whether seeking funding, mentorship, or partnerships.

After the pitch, follow up with a thank-you email, summarizing key points and next steps. A well-executed pitch not only secures funding but also builds relationships that can benefit your business long-term.

CHAPTER XXXIII

Managing Finances

Managing Business Finances: The Importance of Accurate Bookkeeping

Effective financial management begins with accurate record-keeping. A well-structured bookkeeping system ensures transparency, accountability, and a clear understanding of a business's financial health. By tracking income, expenses, assets, and liabilities, businesses can make informed financial decisions, manage cash flow efficiently, and maintain compliance with tax regulations.

Understanding Double-Entry Bookkeeping

A reliable accounting method, double-entry bookkeeping, records every financial transaction in two accounts—one as a debit and the other as a credit—ensuring that the fundamental accounting equation (Assets = Liabilities + Equity) remains balanced. This method helps detect errors and maintain accuracy in financial statements.

How It Works:

- Debits record money entering the business, increasing assets (e.g., cash, inventory).
- Credits record money leaving the business, increasing liabilities or equity (e.g., loan payments, sales revenue).

Example: If a business purchases inventory worth $200 on credit, the transaction is recorded as:

- Debit Inventory (Asset): +$200 (since the business now owns stock).
- Credit Accounts Payable (Liability): +$200 (reflecting the amount owed to the supplier).

This ensures that the books remain balanced and accurate.

Financial Reports for Better Decision-Making

A well-maintained bookkeeping system allows businesses to generate essential financial reports, including:

- Balance Sheet: Shows assets, liabilities, and equity.
- Profit & Loss Statement: Tracks revenue, expenses, and profitability.
- Cash Flow Statement: Records money flowing in and out of the business.

Regularly reviewing these reports provides insights into financial performance, budgeting, and investment planning, ensuring that businesses remain profitable and sustainable.

Keeping Transactions Organized

Every business transaction affects at least two accounts and must be recorded accurately to maintain balanced books. For example, a $500 sale would be recorded as:

- Debit Cash/Accounts Receivable (Asset): +$500 (reflecting received income).
- Credit Sales Revenue (Equity): +$500 (recognizing earned revenue).

Maintaining accurate financial records not only supports daily operations but also simplifies tax preparation, helps secure loans or investments, and prevents financial discrepancies.

Ensuring Accuracy and Compliance

Using accounting software, hiring a professional accountant, or conducting regular reconciliations can streamline bookkeeping and ensure compliance with tax laws. Whether managing accounts manually or through software, keeping financial records balanced and updated is crucial for making informed business decisions and ensuring long-term financial stability.

CHAPTER XXXIV

Tax

Understanding Business Taxation: Compliance and Financial Planning

Managing taxes effectively is essential for business owners to ensure compliance, avoid penalties, and optimize financial planning. Understanding different tax structures, calculating obligations, and setting aside funds for tax payments help businesses stay financially stable.

How Business Taxes Work

The taxes a business owes depend on its structure—whether it's a sole proprietorship, partnership, or company. Each structure has its own tax responsibilities, and choosing the right one impacts overall financial management.

Business Income and Tax Calculation

Taxes are calculated based on the business's profitability, meaning revenue and expenses must be tracked carefully.

1. Revenue (Turnover): The total income earned from sales or services.
2. Expenses: Costs of running the business, including rent, wages, materials, and operational costs.

3. Gross Profit: Revenue minus expenses; the amount subject to taxation.
4. Net Profit: The remaining profit after taxes, which can be reinvested or distributed as dividends.

Tracking monthly profitability and setting aside tax reserves ensures businesses can meet tax obligations without financial strain.

Common Business Taxes

- Sales Tax / VAT: A tax collected from customers at the point of sale. Businesses must register for VAT if revenue exceeds a threshold and remit collected tax to the government.
- Income Tax: Sole proprietors and business partners pay personal income tax on their share of business profits.
- Company Taxes: Registered companies pay corporate tax on profits, often at a flat rate. Directors and employees pay separate income tax on salaries or dividends.
- Local Business Taxes: In some regions, businesses pay additional taxes based on location, commercial property usage, or industry regulations.

Tax Compliance and Responsibilities

Businesses must register for taxes, maintain records, and file annual tax returns. Hiring an accountant can help ensure compliance, maximize deductions, and streamline the tax filing process. Understanding terms like capital gains tax (CGT), tax thresholds, and dividend taxation also helps in managing profits and investments wisely.

By staying informed and proactive, business owners can budget effectively, meet tax deadlines, and keep their finances in good order while ensuring long-term growth.

CHAPTER XXXV

Bank Account

Setting Up a Business Bank Account: A Smart Financial Move

While not always mandatory, having a separate business bank account is a wise decision for managing finances efficiently. It provides access to specialized banking services, clearer financial records, and credibility when dealing with customers, suppliers, and financial institutions.

Key Benefits of a Business Bank Account

- Separation of Finances: Keeps personal and business transactions distinct, simplifying accounting and tax reporting.
- Improved Cash Flow Management: Allows better tracking of income, expenses, and regular payments.
- Payment Processing: Enables acceptance of credit/debit card transactions and online payments.
- Access to Business Banking Services: Offers features such as overdrafts, loans, currency exchange, and financing options.
- Credit History Building: Establishes a financial track record, making it easier to secure future funding or business credit lines.

Traditional Banks vs. Fintech Alternatives

In addition to traditional banks, fintech institutions provide automated financial solutions for businesses focused on online transactions, global payments, or multi-currency operations. The right choice depends on business needs, including transaction volume, digital banking preferences, and financial services required.

Questions to Consider Before Opening a Business Account

Choosing the right banking partner is crucial. Before proceeding, ask the following:

- How long does it take to open an account? Some banks take weeks to process applications, while fintech providers may offer faster access.
- Are there introductory offers? Some banks provide free banking for a limited period, but compare long-term fees.
- What are the monthly and transaction charges? Review costs for account maintenance, deposits, withdrawals, and online payments to avoid hidden fees.
- What documents are required? Typically, businesses need proof of identity, address, and company registration documents to comply with regulations.
- Does the bank offer a dedicated relationship manager? Having a personal banking contact can provide tailored financial advice and support.
- Does the bank provide business advice? Some banks offer market insights, networking events, and

investment guidance for growing businesses.

- Is overdraft access available? Overdrafts help manage cash flow fluctuations, but terms and fees should be reviewed.
- How quickly are deposits processed? Faster processing ensures smoother financial operations and improves liquidity.

Choosing the Right Business Account

Before opening an account, ensure you:

- Gather all required documents to expedite the process.
- Compare banking options based on fees, services, and customer support.
- Select an account that aligns with your current business needs and future growth plans.

By carefully evaluating options, business owners can secure a banking solution that enhances financial management, operational efficiency, and long-term stability.

CHAPTER XXXVI

Insurance

Securing Your Business: Managing Risks and Insurance Coverage

All businesses face risks, but identifying and managing them effectively can help minimize losses and ensure long-term stability. A well-planned risk management strategy, combined with the right business insurance, protects against unexpected financial burdens.

Assessing and Managing Risks

The first step in risk management is conducting a risk assessment. List potential risks, evaluate their likelihood and severity, and decide how to handle them:

- Avoid: Change processes or suppliers to eliminate risks.
- Minimize: Implement measures to reduce the impact or probability of risks.
- Accept: Acknowledge manageable risks and monitor them closely.
- Transfer: Use insurance to shift the financial burden of risks to a third party.

Types of Business Insurance

Choosing the right insurance depends on your industry, operations, and location. Here are key types of business insurance to consider:

- Business Interruption Insurance: Covers lost income if your business is forced to shut down due to fire, natural disasters, or other emergencies.
- Product Liability Insurance: Protects against claims from defective products that cause injury or damage.
- Legal Protection Insurance: Covers legal expenses and defense costs in case of lawsuits.
- Employers' Liability Insurance: Required in many regions, this covers workplace injuries and illnesses affecting employees.
- Stock and Contents Insurance: Protects inventory, equipment, and assets from theft, fire, or vandalism.
- Buildings Insurance: Covers damage to business premises from flooding, fire, or other disasters.
- Public Liability Insurance: Protects against claims from third parties for injuries or property damage caused by your business.
- Professional Liability Insurance: Essential for service-based businesses, covering claims of negligence, errors, or financial losses due to your services.
- Cyber Liability Insurance: Protects against data breaches, cyberattacks, and loss of sensitive information.
- Vehicle Insurance: Covers business vehicles for damage, theft, or liability.
- Directors and Officers Insurance (D&O): Shields company leaders from personal liability lawsuits related to business decisions.

Choosing the Right Insurance for Your Business

To ensure adequate coverage, consider:

- Industry-Specific Risks: Identify potential threats based on your business type.
- Legal Requirements: Check if certain insurance policies are mandatory in your location.
- Expert Advice: Consult an insurance broker for tailored recommendations.

Final Thoughts

Risk is unavoidable, but having the right insurance in place ensures financial protection. As your business grows, reassess insurance needs regularly to stay adequately covered. A proactive approach to risk management strengthens your business's resilience, allowing you to focus on growth and success.

CHAPTER XXXVII

Licenses and Permits

Ensuring Legal Compliance and Protecting Intellectual Property

For a business to operate successfully and securely, obtaining the necessary licenses and protecting intellectual property (IP) are essential. Legal compliance helps avoid penalties, fines, and legal disputes, while IP protection ensures business innovations remain exclusive and competitive.

Securing Business Licenses and Permits

Certain business activities require specific permits or government-issued licenses, such as those for exporting goods, selling food, or offering professional services. Failing to comply with these requirements can result in legal action, fines, or operational shutdowns. Business owners should thoroughly research their industry's regulations and secure all necessary permits before launching or expanding operations.

Protecting Your Intellectual Property (IP)

Intellectual property includes innovations, brand names, artistic works, and proprietary business knowledge. Without proper protection, competitors can copy or steal valuable ideas, potentially harming business growth. IP protection methods vary based on the type of creation, and in some cases, multiple forms of protection may be necessary.

Types of Intellectual Property Protections

- Patents: Protect new inventions, processes, and designs, granting exclusive rights to use, make, or sell the innovation for up to 20 years.
- Trademarks: Safeguard brand names, logos, and symbols that identify a business's products or services, preventing confusion in the marketplace.
- Copyrights: Automatically apply to original creative works, such as books, films, software, and music, ensuring creators control reproduction and distribution.
- Registered Designs: Secure the visual appearance of products, including shape, color, or texture, preventing unauthorized replication.
- Trade Secrets: Protect confidential business information, such as formulas, proprietary methods, or recipes, as long as they remain undisclosed.

Multiple Layers of Protection

Businesses often require a combination of IP protections to fully safeguard their assets. For instance, a new product might be secured through patents (for its function), trademarks (for branding), and copyrights (for marketing materials). Conducting IP research ensures that ideas do not infringe on existing rights, reducing legal risks.

Final Considerations

Securing business licenses and intellectual property rights not only provides legal protection but also enhances credibility and competitive positioning. Regularly reviewing legal compliance and IP strategies ensures businesses remain secure, innovative, and well-protected against potential risks.

CHAPTER XXXVIII

Environment

Building a Sustainable Business: Reducing Environmental Impact

Emphasizing sustainability in business does more than help combat climate change—it enhances brand reputation, builds trust with customers, and reduces operational costs. Consumers, employees, and stakeholders increasingly support eco-conscious businesses, making sustainability a valuable competitive advantage.

Steps to Creating a Greener Business

Sustainability efforts can be broken into three key areas: Resources, Operations, and Products.

- Resources: Choose responsibly sourced materials, such as Fair Trade products or recycled fabrics, to minimize environmental harm.
- Operations: Optimize energy use, reduce waste, and adopt eco-friendly production methods to lower costs and regulatory risks.
- Products: Reduce waste by using recyclable, compostable, or reusable packaging and offering refill programs.

Supporting Local and Reducing Waste

Sourcing from local suppliers reduces transportation emissions while strengthening community ties. Businesses can further reduce their carbon footprint by adopting energy-efficient operations, such as electric vehicles for deliveries or well-insulated buildings.

Plastic waste remains a global issue, but businesses can help by choosing recyclable materials and exploring plastic reuse innovations, such as turning waste into fabric, fuel, or building materials.

Compliance and Eco-Certifications

Environmental regulations mandate responsible waste management, emissions control, and pollution reduction. Staying compliant helps avoid penalties and legal issues. Voluntary eco-certifications, such as organic or sustainable product certifications, further boost credibility and attract environmentally conscious customers.

Long-Term Benefits of Sustainability

A commitment to sustainability reduces costs, builds customer loyalty, and future-proofs businesses against evolving environmental regulations. By integrating green practices into business strategy, companies stay competitive, foster community support, and contribute to a healthier planet.

CHAPTER XXXIX

Integrity

Running a Business with Integrity: The Foundation of Ethical Success

Operating ethically is more than meeting legal requirements—it's about building trust with employees, customers, suppliers, and the community. Ethical business practices create a strong reputation, long-term relationships, and sustainable growth.

Ensuring Workplace Integrity

- Fair Treatment & Inclusivity: Provide equal opportunities, ensure a safe workplace, and support diversity and respect.
- Employee Well-Being: Offer competitive wages, benefits, career development, and a healthy work-life balance.
- Leading by Example: Business leaders must demonstrate integrity, open communication, and ethical decision-making.

Building Ethical Business Relationships

- Ethical Sourcing: Partner with suppliers who uphold fair labor and sustainable sourcing.
- Local Sourcing: Support local economies and reduce environmental impact through local partnerships.
- Honest Communication: Be transparent with customers, provide accurate product information, and address concerns responsibly.
- Customer Engagement: Build relationships by valuing customer feedback and ensuring trust.

Community and Environmental Responsibility

- Giving Back: Engage in charitable efforts, sponsor community events, and support social causes.
- Reducing Environmental Impact: Implement waste reduction, energy conservation, and carbon offset programs.
- Sustainable Business Practices: Use eco-friendly packaging, promote recycling, and invest in renewable energy.

Establishing Ethical Business Operations

- Transparency: Maintain ethical marketing, fair pricing, and honest advertising.
- Accountability: Regularly review and improve ethical standards in finance, customer service, and social responsibility.

- Code of Conduct: Define guidelines for customer relations, supplier ethics, environmental sustainability, and compliance.

The Power of Ethical Choices

Consumers increasingly support businesses that prioritize ethics, even if it means paying slightly more. Sourcing from ethically traded suppliers, despite higher costs, builds long-term trust and strengthens brand loyalty.

A well-structured code of conduct reinforces ethical principles, ensuring that employees, suppliers, and business partners remain aligned with core values. By committing to ethical business practices, companies foster sustainability, trust, and long-term success.

CHAPTER XL

Creating Your Business Plan

Developing a Business Plan: Creating a Roadmap for Success

A business plan serves as a structured guide that outlines the objectives, strategies, and financial projections of your business. It not only provides clarity for your entrepreneurial journey but also demonstrates your business's potential to investors, partners, and stakeholders. A well-prepared plan helps secure funding, set clear goals, track progress, and boost confidence in your venture.

Structuring Your Business Plan

A strong business plan should be concise, well-organized, and backed by thorough research. It should clearly define your business model, target market, competitive advantage, operational framework, and financial expectations.

The executive summary is the first section and should briefly introduce your business name, structure, mission, and a compelling elevator pitch. This section should provide a snapshot of your business, summarizing key details like your product or service offering, market positioning, and financial goals.

The next section focuses on business details, including ownership, location, and product descriptions. Highlight what makes your offerings unique and how they meet customer needs. A SWOT analysis can be useful in identifying strengths, weaknesses, opportunities, and threats, helping you strategize for potential challenges.

A well-researched market and competition analysis strengthens your business plan by showcasing an understanding of your industry. Clearly define your target audience, their demographics, and spending habits. Identify your direct and indirect competitors, analyze their strengths and weaknesses, and emphasize what makes your business stand out.

Crafting an Effective Marketing and Sales Strategy

A business cannot thrive without a solid marketing and sales plan. Define how you will attract and retain customers, whether through digital marketing, social media engagement, advertising campaigns, or referral programs. Outline your pricing model and customer acquisition strategy, ensuring that it aligns with your revenue goals and market positioning.

Operational Framework and Financial Projections

The business operations section should explain how your company will function on a daily basis. Address aspects like supply chain management, logistics, and compliance with legal regulations. Ensuring smooth operations is critical to delivering value to customers and sustaining growth.

A financial projection section provides an estimate of expected revenue, costs, and profit margins. Investors will look for realistic sales forecasts, expense breakdowns, and cash flow projections. Demonstrating financial viability with well-calculated projections improves your chances of securing funding.

Transforming Strategy into Action

A business plan serves as the foundation, but an action plan is essential for execution. An action plan details specific steps, deadlines, and responsibilities for achieving business goals. Regular reviews ensure that business strategies remain adaptable to market changes and new opportunities.

For instance, a tour company launching new winter routes might develop a marketing action plan that focuses on social media campaigns, promotional offers, and customer outreach. Each component of the campaign would require a structured timeline, designated responsibilities, and progress tracking to maximize effectiveness.

By integrating a strong business plan with an actionable strategy, entrepreneurs can confidently navigate their growth journey. A well-crafted plan not only enhances credibility among investors but also provides a structured approach to achieving long-term success.

CHAPTER XLI

Understanding Consumer Rights

Understanding Consumer Rights and Business Responsibilities

When starting a business, ensuring compliance with consumer protection laws is essential. Businesses that sell products or services must understand their legal responsibilities toward customers to maintain trust, avoid legal disputes, and provide high-quality offerings. Consumer protection laws safeguard buyers from unfair sales tactics, misleading practices, and substandard products or services.

Selling Products: Consumer Protection Regulations

Consumer laws apply to both physical and digital products, requiring businesses to meet quality standards, provide clear product descriptions, and ensure fair pricing. These regulations protect consumers from faulty, misrepresented, or unsafe products, covering areas such as food safety, electronics, and product labeling. With the rise of e-commerce and cross-border trade, organizations like the International Consumer Protection and Enforcement Network (ICPEN) are working to establish global consumer protection standards, ensuring transparency and fairness in international transactions.

Providing Services: Meeting Legal Standards

Service-based businesses must also adhere to consumer rights laws, ensuring that services are delivered with reasonable care, skill, and within agreed timelines. Industries such as construction, beauty, and home maintenance must comply with laws requiring clear pricing, fair contracts, and service guarantees. If a service does not meet expectations, businesses may be required to redo the service or offer compensation. Addressing complaints effectively not only ensures legal compliance but also helps build long-term customer loyalty.

Key Consumer Rights and Business Compliance

Governments and consumer protection agencies actively enforce consumer rights, ensuring fair treatment in transactions. These rights generally include:

- Quality assurance: Products and services must meet industry standards and function as advertised.
- Fitness for purpose: Items must serve the purpose for which they are sold.
- Transparent pricing: Customers should receive accurate, upfront pricing without hidden fees.
- Fair returns and refunds: Businesses must offer solutions for faulty products, including repairs, replacements, or refunds.
- Delivery standards: Goods and services must be provided within the agreed timeframe.

Consulting local and national consumer protection agencies before launching a business ensures compliance with specific legal requirements. Whether selling retail products or offering professional services, businesses must prioritize consumer rights and ethical practices to maintain credibility, customer trust, and legal security.

CHAPTER XLII

Website

Creating a Website: Building a Strong Online Presence

Establishing a website is a fundamental step in growing your business. A well-designed site enhances credibility, attracts visitors, and provides a platform to showcase your products or services. Thoughtful planning and execution ensure that your website effectively engages your target audience while maintaining a professional and user-friendly design.

Planning Your Website Content

Before designing your website, outline its structure and content strategy. Define its primary purpose—whether it's to sell products, provide information, or engage with customers. Identify your target audience and tailor the content to their needs. Researching competitors can provide insights into effective design elements and content formats, such as instructional videos, blogs, or interactive features.

Selecting a Domain Name

Choosing a domain name is a crucial step in establishing your brand online. The name should be short, memorable, and easy to spell. Avoid numbers or hyphens, as they can confuse users. Incorporating relevant keywords improves search engine optimization (SEO), helping customers find your site. Once you select a domain, check its availability through a domain registrar and secure it before proceeding with development.

Choosing the Right Website Development Method

There are multiple ways to build a website, depending on your technical skills and business needs.

For beginners, website builders like Wix, Squarespace, or Shopify provide an easy-to-use, drag-and-drop interface with pre-designed templates. These platforms are ideal for those who need a functional, visually appealing site without coding experience.

For more flexibility, Content Management Systems (CMS) like WordPress allow for greater customization with themes and plugins. This option suits businesses that require frequent content updates or additional features beyond a basic template.

For complete creative control, building a website from scratch using HTML, CSS, and JavaScript is the most advanced option. This method requires coding expertise but offers the highest level of customization. It is best suited for large-scale or highly specialized websites.

Key Considerations for Website Development

Regardless of the method you choose, design, usability, and functionality must be prioritized. Your website should be clean, easy to navigate, and optimized for mobile devices. Search engine optimization (SEO) helps improve visibility, ensuring your site ranks well on search engines. A fast, responsive, and well-structured site enhances the user experience, encouraging visitors to stay longer and engage with your content.

Ensuring Mobile-Friendliness and Scalability

With mobile browsing accounting for a significant portion of internet traffic, ensuring that your site is responsive across different devices is essential. As your business grows, consider whether your website can easily scale and adapt to new content, products, or features.

Hosting and Performance Optimization

Choosing a reliable web hosting provider impacts site speed and security. Avoid shared hosting services that could slow down your website due to high traffic from other users. Some website builders may not be fully SEO-optimized, so selecting the right hosting and platform ensures better performance.

A website is a powerful tool for business growth. Whether using a website builder, CMS, or custom coding, focus on usability, mobile optimization, and SEO to create a site that enhances brand visibility and customer engagement. Regular updates and improvements will keep your site relevant, ensuring long-term success in the digital marketplace.

CHAPTER XLIII

SEO

Driving Website Traffic: Strategies for Growth

Building an online presence requires more than just launching a website; it demands consistent efforts to attract and retain visitors. A combination of SEO, content marketing, social media engagement, and paid advertising can help businesses increase visibility, generate leads, and boost conversions.

Optimizing for Search Engines (SEO)

SEO is a long-term strategy that helps websites rank higher on search engine results pages (SERPs). The foundation of SEO begins with keyword research, where businesses identify relevant terms that their target audience is searching for. Using tools like Google Keyword Planner or Moz's Keyword Explorer, businesses can find high-ranking keywords and incorporate them naturally into website content.

Effective on-page SEO includes optimizing titles, meta descriptions, headers, and images to improve search visibility. Since mobile-first indexing is now a priority for search engines, ensuring that a website is responsive and loads quickly across all devices is essential. Additionally, technical SEO improvements, such as fixing broken links and optimizing site speed, enhance user experience and ranking potential.

Leveraging Backlinks for Authority

Backlinks—links from other reputable websites—help search engines recognize a website as a credible source. To attract quality backlinks, businesses should create high-value, shareable content such as industry insights, research articles, or case studies. Listing a business in online directories and contributing guest blog posts to authoritative sites also strengthens backlink profiles.

Creating Engaging Content

Quality content keeps visitors on a website and encourages return visits. Regularly publishing blog posts that answer customer questions, offer industry tips, or share success stories can build an engaged audience. Video content, such as tutorials and product demos, can increase engagement, especially when shared on platforms like YouTube. Other formats, such as infographics, podcasts, and downloadable guides, add variety and increase sharing potential.

Maximizing Social Media Impact

Social media platforms provide businesses with direct access to their audience. Setting up business profiles on platforms like Facebook, Instagram, LinkedIn, and Twitter helps establish brand presence. Regular posting, engaging with followers, and sharing website links through stories and bios can direct traffic back to the website.

Using Digital Marketing to Boost Traffic

Strategic email marketing campaigns with newsletters, promotions, and updates keep customers engaged while directing them back to the website. Implementing referral programs encourages existing customers to bring in new visitors, while influencer collaborations expose businesses to new audiences.

Investing in Paid Advertising

While organic methods take time, paid advertising delivers immediate traffic. Running PPC (pay-per-click) campaigns on Google Ads helps target specific keywords, while social media ads on Facebook and Instagram allow businesses to reach defined demographics. Retargeting ads, which display advertisements to past website visitors, help convert leads who didn't take action on their first visit.

Exploring Offline Promotion

Website promotion isn't limited to digital channels. Businesses can include their website URL on business cards, storefront signage, flyers, and vehicle branding to drive traffic from offline interactions.

Tracking and Improving Performance

Understanding website visitors' behavior through cookies, analytics tools, and demographic tracking enables businesses to personalize user experiences. Refining marketing strategies based on customer insights ensures that efforts remain effective.

Growing website traffic requires a blend of SEO, high-quality content, social media presence, and strategic marketing efforts. Consistently applying these methods, monitoring results, and refining strategies will lead to increased engagement, conversions, and long-term business growth.

CHAPTER XLIV

Data

Data Protection: Safeguarding Your Business from Cyber Threats

In an increasingly digital world, protecting business data is a critical priority. Cyber-attacks target businesses of all sizes, and small enterprises are particularly vulnerable due to limited resources and security measures. However, with the right cybersecurity strategies, businesses can effectively minimize risks and safeguard sensitive information without excessive costs.

Building a Cybersecurity Strategy

Investing in basic security tools and allocating a budget for cybersecurity significantly reduces the risk of cyber threats. Antivirus software, firewalls, and regular data backups form the foundation of a strong security system. Cloud storage and external drives provide redundancy, ensuring data remains secure in case of breaches or system failures. Conducting a risk analysis can help identify potential vulnerabilities, allowing businesses to strengthen weak points in their systems.

Essential Cybersecurity Measures

A majority of cyber threats can be prevented by implementing essential security software. Installing and regularly updating firewalls, antivirus programs, and malware detection tools helps block unauthorized access and detect threats before they cause damage. Regular software updates ensure that security patches are applied, closing potential loopholes that attackers might exploit.

Password protection is another key factor—using strong passwords, multi-factor authentication (MFA), and resetting default credentials on all devices adds an extra layer of security. Businesses should also restrict the use of USB drives and memory cards to prevent malware infiltration.

Testing and Updating Security Systems

Cybersecurity is an ongoing process, requiring businesses to regularly test and update security measures. Vulnerability scans help detect weak spots in systems, while penetration testing simulates attacks to evaluate security effectiveness. Employees must be trained to recognize and report suspicious emails, links, and downloads to reduce the risk of phishing attacks.

Cybersecurity Awareness and Employee Training

Human error remains one of the biggest cybersecurity risks. Educating employees on safe browsing habits, phishing threats, and secure password management can prevent accidental breaches. Encouraging staff to be cautious with emails, links, and third-party software downloads strengthens the company's defense against cybercriminals.

Seeking Professional Cybersecurity Advice

For businesses unsure about security best practices, consulting cybersecurity professionals or government resources can provide valuable insights. Many organizations offer free guidance on risk management and security enhancements tailored for small businesses.

Protecting Business Reputation and Customer Trust

Beyond preventing financial losses, cybersecurity safeguards a business's reputation and maintains customer trust. Data breaches can lead to legal consequences, particularly regarding customer data protection laws. Implementing robust security measures ensures compliance with information security regulations and demonstrates a commitment to protecting client information.

Regularly updating security protocols and staying ahead of evolving cyber threats is essential for long-term business stability. By investing in cybersecurity, businesses can reduce risks, protect data, and create a secure digital environment for growth and success.

CHAPTER XLV

Ideal Talent

Finding the Right Talent for Your Business

Attracting and retaining top talent is a key factor in driving business success. Whether hiring full-time employees, outsourcing work, or utilizing freelancers, selecting the right individuals ensures efficiency and competitiveness. Understanding your hiring needs, identifying effective recruitment strategies, and maintaining a strong company reputation all contribute to securing the best candidates.

Assessing Hiring Needs

Before beginning recruitment, analyze the workload, required skills, and business objectives. Permanent hires involve long-term commitments, including recruitment, training, and benefits. If the work is temporary or highly specialized, outsourcing to freelancers or agencies can be a cost-effective alternative. For seasonal or project-based work, fixed-term contracts offer flexibility without long-term financial burdens.

Attracting the Right Candidates

A company's reputation and work culture significantly impact its ability to attract skilled professionals. Seeking feedback from current employees, analyzing industry job postings, and observing successful hiring practices can provide insights into what appeals to job seekers. Authenticity is key—promises made regarding workplace conditions, growth opportunities, and training must be honored to maintain employee satisfaction and reduce turnover.

Effective Methods for Finding Talent

There are multiple ways to identify and recruit top talent, each offering distinct advantages based on the business's size, industry, and hiring needs.

- Referrals from Trusted Contacts: Personal recommendations from colleagues, employees, or business partners often lead to reliable, well-vetted hires who align with company culture.
- Online Job Platforms and Networking Sites: Websites such as LinkedIn, Indeed, and Glassdoor provide access to a broad talent pool, allowing employers to filter candidates by skills, experience, and location.
- Colleges and Universities: Partnering with career services, job placement programs, and internship opportunities helps businesses connect with fresh talent eager to gain experience.
- Recruitment Agencies: While costlier, agencies streamline the hiring process by screening, shortlisting, and conducting initial interviews, saving businesses time and effort.
- Local Job Boards and Community Networks: Posting job openings in libraries, community centers, or local online forums can attract regional talent suited for location-specific roles.

- Industry-Specific Publications and Websites: Advertising in specialized journals, trade magazines, and niche job portals helps attract highly qualified professionals with targeted expertise.

Building a Sustainable Hiring Strategy

Using a mix of recruitment methods ensures diverse and high-quality candidates. Keeping a database of skilled professionals who may be relevant for future positions is a smart way to reduce hiring time when new roles become available. Businesses should remain transparent, patient, and methodical in their hiring decisions to avoid costly recruitment mistakes.

Hiring the right people is an investment in the growth and stability of a business. Rushing into decisions or overpromising can lead to disengagement and turnover, ultimately harming productivity. A well-planned recruitment process, based on business needs and industry best practices, ensures that businesses secure talent that drives long-term success.

CHAPTER XLVI

Hiring Employees

Effective Hiring and Management for Business Growth

Recruiting the right employees requires a thoughtful, structured approach that goes beyond technical skills. Finding candidates with the right knowledge, attitude, and experience can significantly impact your business's success. The hiring process involves careful job role planning, targeted advertising, structured interviews, and informed decision-making to ensure the best fit for your team.

Hiring the Right Candidate

When recruiting, it's essential to assess both technical expertise and personal attributes such as teamwork, problem-solving abilities, and adaptability. Previous experience in a similar business environment can also be a valuable asset. Offering a competitive salary and benefits package attracts high-quality candidates, and researching industry job advertisements can help you determine market standards.

Utilizing multiple recruitment channels, such as job posting websites, professional networks, and employee referrals, increases the chances of finding the best match. Planning ahead—considering your hiring budget, timeline, and onboarding process—ensures a smooth transition for the new hire.

It is also important to ensure that interview questions remain professional and non-discriminatory. Avoid personal questions related to marital status, religion, or health conditions that could result in legal complications. Keeping questions relevant to job responsibilities ensures a fair and transparent hiring process.

When to Consider Hiring a Manager

As your business expands, managing all operations alone can become overwhelming. While a manager may not be necessary in the early stages, they can streamline workflows, improve efficiency, and provide leadership as the business grows.

A manager's role typically includes overseeing projects, managing staff, organizing resources, and maintaining order within the organization. Strong leadership and communication skills are crucial for ensuring smooth day-to-day operations and fostering a motivated and high-performing workforce.

The Value of Hiring a Manager

Although hiring a manager involves additional salary expenses, the benefits often outweigh the costs. A skilled manager can boost productivity, enhance team morale, and optimize resource allocation, leading to overall business growth and profitability. If hiring a full-time manager seems financially challenging, starting with a temporary or part-time manager can help assess their impact and suitability for your business.

Planning for Future Growth

Even if your business is currently manageable without additional leadership, considering future expansion plans, product launches, or marketing campaigns is essential. Identifying tasks that require expert oversight and planning ahead ensures that when the time comes, you can recruit the right manager with the necessary skills and experience.

Finding the Right Manager

An effective manager should bring new ideas, challenge inefficient methods, and thrive in a fast-paced environment. Look for individuals who are versatile, proactive, and capable of working independently while coaching and inspiring their team. Trustworthiness and strong interpersonal skills are essential, as a good manager should be able to build loyalty, foster a positive work culture, and drive business success.

Investing in talent acquisition and leadership development sets the stage for long-term business sustainability. Whether hiring employees or bringing in a manager, prioritizing skills, adaptability, and alignment with company values ensures that your business is positioned for growth, stability, and continued success.

CHAPTER XLVII

Customer Data System

Implementing a Customer Data System for Business Growth

Understanding customer behavior is essential for delivering exceptional service and fostering long-term relationships. A Customer Relationship Management (CRM) system streamlines this process by gathering, organizing, and analyzing customer data, enabling businesses to improve customer interactions and drive growth. By implementing a CRM, businesses can personalize marketing efforts, optimize service delivery, and enhance customer retention.

Collecting Customer Data

To maximize the benefits of a CRM system, businesses must collect data through various touchpoints. A well-designed website acts as a primary source of customer insights, capturing user behavior through sign-ups, inquiries, and browsing patterns. Social media engagement provides real-time feedback, allowing businesses to track audience preferences and interests. Email communications, such as newsletters and promotional offers, further enhance customer engagement while providing valuable data on open rates and responses.

Encouraging customer referrals and loyalty programs reveals which customers are most engaged, helping businesses identify their most valuable clients. Running promotional campaigns and special offers provides insights into purchasing trends and demand patterns. Direct face-to-face interactions at events or in-store visits allow businesses to gain deeper insights into customer needs, while effective complaint resolution and follow-ups highlight areas for improvement.

Using CRM Data for Business Success

A CRM system organizes customer data to identify buying patterns, preferences, and peak engagement times. By analyzing these insights, businesses can refine their marketing strategies, ensuring they target the right audience with relevant content and offers. Tracking market trends and product popularity allows businesses to adapt their offerings and capitalize on emerging opportunities.

CRM systems also help in measuring marketing effectiveness by analyzing how customers respond to campaigns. If a promotion underperforms, businesses can adjust their approach based on data-driven insights. Moreover, by identifying high-value customers, businesses can develop tailored offers and services that encourage repeat purchases, boosting profitability.

Enhancing Competitive Advantage with CRM

Beyond improving marketing and sales, a CRM system strengthens overall customer relationships by ensuring businesses can anticipate and meet client expectations. By leveraging data effectively, companies can create a more personalized experience, increasing customer satisfaction and brand loyalty.

CRM software also enhances operational efficiency, allowing teams to track interactions, streamline communication, and automate tasks like follow-ups and reminders. As customer expectations continue to evolve, businesses that invest in CRM technology gain a competitive advantage by offering data-driven, customer-centric experiences.

Delaying the adoption of a CRM system may seem cost-effective in the short term, but businesses that prioritize customer insights position themselves for long-term success. Investing in a CRM system ensures that businesses can track customer needs, refine marketing efforts, and enhance service delivery, ultimately leading to sustained growth and stronger customer loyalty.

CHAPTER XLVIII

Getting Ready for Launch

Prelaunch Strategy: Setting the Stage for a Successful Business Launch

Launching a business requires more than just having a product or service ready—it demands a strategic prelaunch phase to ensure everything is optimized before going live. This stage is critical for testing, refining, and building anticipation to maximize impact on launch day.

Prelaunch Preparation Checklist

1. Refining Your Product or Service
   Before launch, ensure that your product or service functions flawlessly. Conduct final testing to identify and resolve any issues. Getting feedback from test users helps refine the offering and ensures customer satisfaction from day one.
2. Testing Website Performance
   If your business has an online presence, your website must be fully functional, mobile-friendly, and optimized for speed. Test all links, checkout processes, and loading times to prevent technical issues that could frustrate potential customers.
3. Building Publicity and Awareness
   Generating buzz before the official launch is key to driving traffic and sales. Engaging with journalists,

influencers, and industry bloggers ahead of time helps build credibility and early exposure. Personalizing outreach messages increases the chances of coverage.

4. Finalizing a Marketing Plan

   A structured marketing strategy ensures your promotional efforts align with your launch timeline. Identify the best channels (social media, email campaigns, paid ads) for reaching your audience. Having a clear promotional calendar helps execute campaigns effectively.

5. Creating a Launch Timeline

   A detailed launch timeline keeps everything organized, ensuring events, promotions, and press releases happen on schedule. Conducting a trial run before launch helps identify potential challenges and allows for necessary adjustments.

Fine-Tuning for Success

A prelaunch phase isn't just about planning; it's about testing and adjusting. Seeking feedback from potential customers, industry peers, and personal networks provides valuable insights into branding, messaging, and overall business appeal. Engaging with your target audience on social media, online forums, or landing pages can help validate demand before going live.

Spreading the Word with Organic Marketing

A successful business launch doesn't always require a massive budget. Low-cost, organic marketing strategies can effectively generate awareness:

- Networking at Events: Engaging with potential customers at industry meetups, trade shows, and community gatherings boosts brand visibility.
- Leveraging Personal and Professional Contacts: Encouraging friends, family, and colleagues to share your business helps expand reach.
- Creating Valuable Online Content: Video demonstrations, blog posts, and customer testimonials establish credibility and attract organic traffic.
- Active Social Media Presence: Engaging in relevant social media groups, collaborations with influencers, and partnerships with complementary brands enhances visibility.
- Multi-Platform Promotion: Listing your business on directories, marketplaces, and review sites increases exposure.
- Promotional Offers and Giveaways: Running limited-time promotions, referral programs, and contests incentivizes customer engagement and drives sales.

Creative and Consistent Messaging

Marketing should align with your brand's values and goals. A well-crafted campaign, even with minimal resources, can create a strong emotional connection with potential customers. Whether through storytelling, humor, or interactive engagement, creative marketing ensures your business stands out in a crowded marketplace.

By taking the time to test, refine, and strategically promote your business before launch, you increase the likelihood of a smooth, impactful debut that attracts customers and generates momentum for long-term success.

CHAPTER XLIX

Generating Excitement for Your Business

Creating Publicity for Your Business

Generating excitement about your business is key to attracting customers, building a loyal base, and driving sales. While marketing focuses on directly promoting your products or services, public relations (PR) helps establish a positive brand image and increase awareness. Using a mix of digital strategies, local engagement, and creative PR techniques, you can build momentum and ensure your business remains top-of-mind for your audience.

Leveraging Digital Platforms for Visibility

The internet provides cost-effective ways to promote your business and engage with potential customers.

- Build a Website: Your website serves as your digital storefront, providing essential information about your offerings, location, and contact details.
- Utilize Social Media: Platforms like Facebook, Instagram, Twitter, and LinkedIn help connect with audiences. Share business updates, promotions, and success stories to maintain engagement.
- Engage in Online Communities: Participate in local forums, Facebook groups, or business networking sites

to spread awareness about your business.

- Share Authentic Stories: Customers connect with real experiences. Regularly post updates about your business journey, customer testimonials, and company milestones.
- Humanize Your Brand: Introducing yourself and your team through blog posts or social media enhances trust and relatability.

Community Engagement to Build Local Support

People naturally support local businesses, and actively engaging with your community fosters goodwill.

- Host Events or Open Houses: Invite potential customers to visit your business, experience your services, and meet your team.
- Join Business Networks: Being part of local business organizations increases your visibility and allows for networking opportunities.
- Sponsor or Participate in Local Events: Supporting charity events, festivals, or sports teams strengthens your brand's local presence and establishes credibility.

Thinking Creatively for Maximum Impact

Publicity thrives on creativity and uniqueness. Eye-catching, innovative marketing strategies make your business stand out.

- Design Attention-Grabbing Flyers: Distribute well-designed, visually appealing posters or flyers in high-traffic areas and share them online.
- Offer Exclusive or Limited-Time Products: Introduce unique offerings that create demand and encourage customers to try something new.
- Host Engaging Competitions: Running giveaways, social media challenges, or contests boosts interaction and attracts new audiences.

Becoming the Face of Your Brand

As the business owner, you play a vital role in representing your brand. Your passion and knowledge can drive trust and credibility.

- Engage with Local Media: Connect with journalists, bloggers, and news outlets to feature your business in local newspapers, magazines, or online publications.
- Establish Yourself as an Industry Expert: Sharing insights through guest articles, podcasts, or interviews builds authority and attracts attention to your business.
- Speak at Public Events: Attending or hosting industry talks, workshops, or networking meetups raises your profile and positions your brand as a leader in the field.

Mastering Public Relations for Long-Term Success

Public relations is an ongoing effort to define and shape how people perceive your business. Developing a strong, authentic brand identity ensures positive relationships with customers, suppliers, and investors. PR also provides free exposure through media coverage, influencer mentions, and customer word-of-mouth.

Using tools like Google Alerts helps track brand mentions and competitor activities, allowing businesses to refine their strategies. Entering industry awards or local business competitions also enhances credibility and offers additional PR opportunities.

Creating buzz for your business is a mix of strategic marketing, strong PR efforts, and community engagement. Consistency and creativity are essential—regularly sharing updates, participating in events, and fostering customer connections will help your business gain momentum. Whether through organic marketing efforts, collaborations, or press coverage, a well-planned approach ensures that your brand remains visible and continues to grow.

CHAPTER L

Advertising

Maximizing Visibility Through Advertising and Social Media Engagement

Increasing visibility for your business requires a well-balanced approach, combining targeted advertising and social media engagement. Choosing the right advertising channels and social platforms ensures your efforts reach the right audience, leading to increased brand awareness, customer engagement, and business growth.

Selecting the Right Advertising Channels

After launching your business and initiating PR efforts, paid advertising can help scale your reach. In a competitive market, selecting the right advertising channels ensures your message reaches the right audience at the right time.

- Traditional Advertising: Print ads, radio, and TV can be effective for targeting older demographics, but they often come with higher costs and limited tracking.
- Online Advertising: Platforms like Google Ads, Facebook Ads, and Instagram Ads offer affordable and targeted marketing, allowing businesses to track performance and adjust campaigns in real-time.
- Social Media Promotions: Investing in paid social media ads allows you to focus on specific customer demographics based on location, interests, and online

behavior.

- Retargeting Ads: Reach potential customers who have previously visited your website but didn't make a purchase.

Social Media as a Powerful Business Tool

Social media helps businesses build relationships, engage audiences, and drive website traffic. To fully leverage social media, businesses must use the right platforms, post engaging content, and actively interact with their audience.

Optimizing Social Media Engagement for Business Growth

1. Creating and Sharing Engaging Content

Social media thrives on high-quality content. Ensure your posts are visually appealing, informative, and engaging.

- Tailor Content for Each Platform: Adjust posts to fit the style of each social media channel.
- Maintain Brand Consistency: Use a recognizable logo, color scheme, and tone across all platforms.
- Utilize Different Content Formats: Experiment with videos, polls, live streams, infographics, and testimonials to keep audiences engaged.

2. Expanding Reach with Hashtags and Engagement

Visibility increases when more people see and interact with your posts.

- Use Relevant Hashtags: Hashtags help users find your business. Examples: #SmallBusiness, #YourBrandName.
- Encourage Engagement: Ask questions, host giveaways, and prompt users to like, comment, or share.

3. Choosing the Right Social Media Platforms

Not every platform suits every business. Select platforms based on where your customers spend the most time.

- Facebook: Best for engaging content, customer service, and promotions.
- Instagram: Ideal for visual brands like fashion, beauty, and food.
- LinkedIn: Perfect for B2B businesses and professional networking.
- Twitter: Great for updates, promotions, and industry news.
- YouTube: Best for businesses offering tutorials, educational content, or product demonstrations.
- TikTok/Snapchat: Effective for brands targeting younger demographics.

4. Tracking Performance and Refining Strategies

Monitor the impact of social media efforts to determine what works.

- Use Analytics Tools: Platforms like Facebook Insights, Instagram Analytics, and Google Analytics track engagement, clicks, and conversions.
- Respond Professionally: Address negative comments constructively to maintain a positive image.

- Cross-Promotion: Include social media links in email signatures, website footers, and marketing materials.

5. Investing in Social Media Advertising
Paid social media ads allow precise audience targeting.

- Define Target Audiences: Use age, location, shopping habits, and interests to refine your audience.
- Design Eye-Catching Ads: Use compelling visuals and persuasive copy to attract attention.
- Drive Website Traffic: Link ads to your website, product pages, or special offers.

Integrating Social Media with Your Website

Your website should seamlessly connect with your social media accounts.

- Embed Social Feeds: Display recent social media posts on your website.
- Encourage Social Sharing: Add social share buttons on blog posts and product pages.
- Create Exclusive Offers: Provide discounts or promotions for followers to drive engagement.

Engaging with Customers for Business Growth

Social media is a two-way conversation. Engaging with both existing and potential customers builds trust and strengthens relationships.

- Respond to Customer Inquiries Promptly
- Encourage User-Generated Content (UGC) – Share customer testimonials and photos.
- Run Interactive Campaigns – Polls, Q&A sessions, and contests keep your audience engaged.

A well-executed advertising and social media strategy ensures that your business stays visible, attracts new customers, and nurtures long-term relationships. Whether through organic content, targeted ads, or community engagement, consistency and creativity are key to making your brand stand out.

CHAPTER LI

Networking

The Power of Networking for Startup Growth

Networking is a vital tool for any startup owner, providing opportunities to build relationships, gain insights, and secure business partnerships. Establishing strong connections can help your business thrive by increasing awareness, generating leads, and opening doors to new opportunities.

The Value of In-Person Networking

While virtual meetings via platforms like Zoom, Microsoft Teams, and Skype make global networking more accessible, in-person interactions remain irreplaceable. Face-to-face meetings foster trust, credibility, and deeper connections that digital interactions can't fully replicate.

Attending industry events, trade shows, networking groups, and business conferences allows you to meet potential clients, investors, and mentors in an authentic setting. Personal interactions help you understand body language, tone, and emotions, making it easier to establish meaningful relationships.

Building and Maintaining Strong Business Relationships

Networking isn't just about expanding your contact list; it's about nurturing and maintaining valuable relationships over time. Organizing your contacts into two categories can help streamline engagement:

1. Target Connections – Potential partners, investors, or customers who could provide business growth opportunities.
2. Existing Network – Relationships you've already built, including clients, colleagues, and mentors, who can offer continued support and collaboration.

Regular communication is key to keeping relationships active and meaningful. Engage with contacts through emails, phone calls, coffee meetings, or casual check-ins to exchange ideas, offer support, or share industry insights.

Effective Networking Strategies

To maximize your networking efforts, follow these best practices:

- Dress Appropriately – Match your attire to the event's setting to feel confident and make a professional impression.
- Listen More Than You Speak – Paying attention to others' needs helps identify common interests and collaboration opportunities.
- Prioritize Relationship-Building Over Sales – Genuine connections lead to long-term opportunities; avoid focusing solely on pitching your products or services.
- Exchange Business Cards – A well-designed business card with your logo, website, and contact details leaves

a lasting impression.
- Follow Up Promptly – Send a follow-up email or LinkedIn connection request within a few days to keep the conversation going.

Leveraging Your Network for Business Growth

- Maintain Trust – Always follow through on promises, whether it's sharing an article, making an introduction, or providing business advice.
- Stay Engaged – Keep in touch with your network by sharing updates, product launches, and industry insights.
- Ask for Feedback – Your contacts can provide valuable insights, mentorship, and even become your first customers.

A strong, well-nurtured network can provide partnerships, mentorship, investment opportunities, and customer referrals. By focusing on authentic engagement, mutual support, and consistent follow-ups, networking can become one of the most powerful tools for your business's long-term success.

CHAPTER LII

Managing Your Business

Fostering Customer Loyalty Through Meaningful Engagement

Building customer loyalty is essential for sustaining long-term business success. Loyal customers provide consistent revenue, help weather market fluctuations, and serve as ambassadors for your brand by recommending your products or services to others. Strengthening this loyalty requires a combination of exceptional service, personalized engagement, and value-driven experiences.

Creating an Emotional Connection

Customer loyalty is built not just on the quality of products or services but also on how customers feel about your brand. Providing engaging, informative, and inspiring content helps nurture this connection. Regular updates, behind-the-scenes insights, and educational materials can make customers feel more involved, encouraging them to stay engaged and return.

Enhancing the Customer Experience

A seamless and enjoyable customer journey fosters loyalty. Simplifying the purchasing process, ensuring clear product information, and maintaining a reliable delivery system help customers feel valued. After-sales service plays a crucial role—resolving issues quickly, offering returns or replacements when necessary, and providing proactive support build trust and encourage repeat business.

Managing Expectations and Delivering Consistency

Clear communication is key to avoiding dissatisfaction. Customers appreciate transparency about delivery times, product quality, and service commitments. Setting realistic expectations and consistently meeting them strengthens trust in your brand. A business that repeatedly delivers on promises becomes a go-to choice for customers.

Exceptional Customer Service as a Loyalty Driver

A business that prioritizes personalized service, quick responses, and customer satisfaction stands out. Thoughtful interactions—such as addressing customers by name, tailoring solutions to their needs, and following up on purchases—create a lasting impression. Going beyond expectations, whether by offering exclusive perks or simply being attentive, makes customers feel valued and strengthens their emotional bond with the brand.

Encouraging Referrals and Word-of-Mouth Marketing

Loyal customers often become enthusiastic brand advocates. Providing incentives for referrals, such as discounts or special offers, can turn satisfied customers into active promoters of your business. Encouraging online reviews and testimonials also builds credibility, as potential customers are more likely to trust peer recommendations.

Leveraging Customer Feedback for Continuous Improvement

Gathering and acting on customer feedback helps refine your offerings and enhances loyalty. Using surveys, live chat, website analytics, and direct conversations allows businesses to understand customer needs better. Engaging with both positive and negative reviews shows responsiveness and a commitment to improving service quality.

Strengthening Customer Bonds for Long-Term Success

In an era where customers have endless options, businesses must go beyond transactions and focus on relationships. Creating personalized experiences, rewarding loyalty, and consistently exceeding expectations foster emotional connections that encourage repeat business. Small yet meaningful gestures—such as remembering preferences, offering unexpected perks, or sending thank-you messages—can turn occasional buyers into lifelong supporters. Prioritizing customer satisfaction at every touchpoint ensures a loyal customer base that not only stays but also actively promotes your brand.

CHAPTER LIII

Customer Connections

Nurturing Customer Connections for Long-Term Success

Building lasting relationships with customers is crucial for fostering loyalty, driving repeat business, and generating organic referrals. While every customer interaction holds value, the most dedicated supporters—those who consistently return and advocate for your brand—are key to long-term success. Strengthening these connections requires a thoughtful approach that goes beyond transactions and focuses on engagement, personalized service, and delivering exceptional experiences.

Creating Meaningful Engagement Through Marketing and Communication

Attracting and retaining customers starts with targeted marketing. Understanding your audience's needs and preferences allows you to craft messages that resonate with them. Instead of broad, generic advertising, focus on personalized campaigns that highlight the unique benefits of your products or services. Once you've captured interest, maintaining consistent communication keeps customers engaged. Email newsletters, social media interactions, and personalized messages help reinforce connections and keep your brand top of mind.

Delivering Quality and Reliability to Build Trust

Customers remain loyal when they can rely on your business to consistently provide value. High-quality products and services, backed by excellent customer support, set the foundation for long-term trust. A seamless and dependable experience—whether through timely deliveries, responsive customer service, or reliable performance—encourages customers to return. Ensuring consistency across all touchpoints reassures customers that they can depend on your brand.

Strengthening Bonds Through Customer Support and Personalized Service

Exceptional customer service goes beyond resolving issues—it's about making customers feel valued. Personalized interactions, thoughtful follow-ups, and attentive aftercare reinforce a positive relationship. Offering guarantees or extended support shows confidence in your products while reassuring customers that their satisfaction matters. Small gestures, such as remembering customer preferences or providing exclusive updates, create a more personalized experience and deepen loyalty.

Encouraging Loyalty Through Rewards and Exclusive Offers

Loyalty programs are a powerful tool for keeping customers engaged. Offering personalized rewards, early access to new products, or referral incentives encourages repeat purchases while strengthening the emotional connection to your brand. A well-designed loyalty program should provide genuine value—whether through discounts, VIP experiences, or special promotions—so that customers feel appreciated and motivated to continue their relationship with your business.

Building Customer Relationships Over Time

Developing strong customer relationships is a gradual process that evolves in stages. Initially, a prospective customer becomes aware of your brand, and their first purchase introduces them to your products or services. If their experience is positive, they return as regular buyers. Over time, a valued customer feels a deeper connection, choosing your business over competitors. Ultimately, the most engaged customers become advocates, enthusiastically recommending your business to others and playing a crucial role in attracting new customers.

Enhancing Customer Experience and Retention

Ensuring a positive customer experience requires continuous effort. Engaging customers through multiple channels, both online and offline, strengthens bonds and fosters brand loyalty. Leveraging customer data allows for more personalized interactions, tailored product recommendations, and customized offers. The goal is not just to meet expectations but to exceed them—whether through superior service, exclusive perks, or unexpected gestures that make customers feel valued.

The Power of Customer Service and Attention to Detail

A well-crafted website or stylish branding may draw attention, but customers ultimately value how they are treated. A business that listens, responds, and genuinely cares about its customers stands out. Regularly evaluating customer interactions and seeking feedback ensures that service remains aligned with their expectations. Paying attention to the small details—whether it's a handwritten thank-you note, prompt responses, or a seamless checkout experience—leaves a lasting impression.

Creating a Customer-Centric Business

Loyalty is not just about transactions; it's about relationships. By prioritizing customer needs, maintaining open communication, and consistently delivering quality, businesses can turn occasional buyers into lifelong advocates. Whether through personalized service, engaging content, or thoughtful loyalty programs, every interaction is an opportunity to reinforce trust and strengthen customer bonds. A customer-centric approach ensures that your business is not just a choice but a preferred and trusted partner for your audience.

CHAPTER LIV

Collaborating with Other Businesses

Building Strong Business Relationships for Long-Term Success

New business owners can greatly benefit from cultivating strong relationships with suppliers and collaborating with complementary businesses. These partnerships can provide access to new customers, strengthen business operations, and create long-term stability.

The Value of Collaboration

Partnerships with other businesses can enhance your start-up by filling gaps in your business model, addressing weaknesses, or expanding your market reach. For example, a cell phone repair business partnering with a retailer can attract customers who need repair services while buying accessories. Start-ups offering innovative products might also attract support from established companies. Collaboration fosters the exchange of ideas, provides new learning experiences, and strengthens business networks. Moreover, developing strong supplier relationships ensures mutual long-term support and reliability in sourcing essential products or services.

Establishing Alliances That Work

With the ease of online networking, finding potential business partners has never been simpler. However, before committing to a partnership, open discussions and clear communication of goals are necessary to ensure a shared vision. While formal contracts may not always be required, having a written agreement outlining objectives, expectations, and responsibilities minimizes misunderstandings and ensures smooth collaboration.

There are two primary types of alliances:

- Horizontal Alliances involve partnerships between businesses in the same industry, often former competitors who decide to work together for mutual gain.
- Vertical Alliances connect businesses at different levels of the supply chain, such as a manufacturer partnering with a distributor or supplier.

Types of Business Partnerships

A well-planned business alliance can provide numerous advantages, including access to resources, increased market reach, and enhanced credibility. However, selecting the right partners is crucial to ensuring success.

1. Strategic Business Partnerships

Business partnerships are most effective when they bring additional value to both parties. Whether teaming up with a complementary business to cross-promote services or working with an expert in a different field, well-structured partnerships drive business growth.

- Choosing the Right Partner: Select businesses that align with your goals, values, and customer base. Look beyond immediate benefits and consider long-term potential.
- Clarifying Expectations: Clearly outline roles, contributions, and expectations for each partner. Define measurable outcomes to track success.
- Maintaining Open Communication: Regular discussions help resolve any issues before they escalate and keep both parties aligned with shared objectives.
- Avoiding Common Pitfalls: Don't rush into partnerships without thorough evaluation. Choose partners based on compatibility rather than size or convenience, and resolve conflicts quickly to maintain a strong relationship.

2. Supplier Relationships

Reliable suppliers play a critical role in business operations, influencing product quality, delivery timelines, and overall efficiency. Establishing a strong relationship with suppliers ensures smooth transactions and better business outcomes.

- Building Trust: Developing a strong rapport with suppliers fosters reliability and better service. Long-term partnerships can lead to better pricing, priority service, and exclusive deals.
- Effective Communication: Keeping suppliers informed about order changes, payment timelines, or expected

fluctuations in demand minimizes disruptions.

- Negotiating Fair Terms: While securing the best deal is important, ensuring that both parties benefit from the agreement strengthens the relationship. Paying on time and sticking to agreed terms enhances credibility.
- Avoiding Supplier Issues: Never cancel large orders at the last minute, as this strains the relationship. Likewise, avoid using one supplier's quote to negotiate lower prices with another—this damages trust and can lead to losing a key supplier.

The Key to Successful Business Alliances

The foundation of any successful partnership or supplier relationship is mutual respect, clear communication, and aligned business goals. Carefully selecting the right partners, ensuring that both sides benefit, and maintaining transparency will lead to stronger, more productive collaborations. Whether working with suppliers, business partners, or industry peers, fostering long-term relationships will contribute significantly to your business's stability and growth.

CHAPTER LV

Marketing to Sales

Maximizing Marketing Effectiveness: Turning Effort into Sales

Marketing is a crucial investment for any business, but ensuring that it leads to tangible sales results is key to long-term success. Understanding where your customers are coming from and which marketing strategies drive the most conversions allows you to focus on the efforts that truly matter.

Evaluating Marketing Performance

A well-structured approach helps in tracking sales effectiveness and optimizing marketing efforts. To ensure your marketing strategies are converting into revenue, it's essential to assess each stage of the customer journey, from awareness to purchase.

Understanding Your Market and Customers

Effective marketing begins with thorough research. Knowing who your ideal customers are, their preferences, and their buying behaviors allows you to tailor campaigns that resonate with them. Market research also helps identify trends and opportunities, ensuring that your product or service remains relevant.

Creating Targeted Campaigns

Personalization is critical in modern marketing. Messages that directly address customer pain points and offer solutions are more likely to engage audiences. Adjusting product features, pricing strategies, and promotional offers to align with consumer expectations increases the likelihood of conversion.

Optimizing the Sales Process

Once marketing efforts drive potential customers to your business, ensuring a seamless purchasing experience is essential. A complicated checkout process, unclear pricing, or limited payment options can deter sales. Streamlining these elements ensures customers complete their transactions effortlessly.

Providing Exceptional Customer Service

Marketing isn't just about attracting new customers—it's also about retaining them. Exceptional customer service fosters loyalty, leading to repeat purchases and positive word-of-mouth referrals. Quick responses to inquiries, personalized interactions, and exceeding expectations all contribute to customer satisfaction.

Using Data to Improve Marketing Strategies

Regularly analyzing customer feedback, sales trends, and market conditions enables businesses to refine their marketing strategies. Staying adaptable and continuously optimizing campaigns based on real data helps maintain a competitive edge.

Measuring Success: Sales Tracking and ROI Analysis

Tracking sales performance is crucial to determine the effectiveness of your marketing efforts. Here's how businesses can analyze their marketing investments:

Identifying the Best Marketing Channels

Determine where your customers are coming from—whether it's social media, search engines, email campaigns, or referrals. Identifying the most effective channels allows businesses to allocate their budgets strategically.

Calculating Return on Investment (ROI)

To measure ROI, compare the revenue generated by marketing efforts with the total amount spent. This helps assess whether a campaign is cost-effective or needs adjustment.

Customer Acquisition Cost (CAC) vs. Customer Lifetime Value (CLV)

Comparing how much it costs to acquire a customer (CAC) against their expected lifetime spending (CLV) determines whether marketing strategies are sustainable. If CAC is consistently higher than CLV, adjustments are needed to improve profitability.

Tracking Key Sales Metrics

Keeping a detailed record of sales over different time periods provides insights into purchasing patterns. Businesses should monitor:

- Daily, weekly, and monthly sales trends.
- Best-selling products or services.
- Sales from new versus returning customers.
- Revenue generated by different marketing channels.
- Conversion rates from ad clicks to completed purchases.

Turning Insights into Action

Marketing should not be a one-time effort but an ongoing process of learning and refinement. By continuously analyzing sales data, businesses can make informed decisions about where to invest their marketing budget. Whether through digital advertising, organic content, or referral programs, focusing on what works best ensures maximum profitability and long-term success.

CHAPTER LVI

Business Performance

Sustaining Business Growth and Performance

To ensure long-term success, continuously monitoring and refining your business strategies is essential. Evaluating performance through key metrics allows for data-driven decision-making, while strategic innovation helps maintain momentum and competitive advantage.

Tracking Performance with KPIs

Key Performance Indicators (KPIs) help measure progress in critical business areas, including marketing, sales, and financial health. Selecting relevant KPIs ensures that you focus on metrics that truly impact business success. Regularly reviewing these indicators allows for timely adjustments to strategies, ensuring efficiency and profitability.

A structured SWOT analysis further helps identify internal strengths and weaknesses while recognizing external opportunities and threats. Understanding these factors guides better business decisions, allowing you to reinforce areas of strength while mitigating risks.

Maintaining Momentum

Once a business gains traction, maintaining that momentum requires strategic action. Expanding networks, forming valuable partnerships, and refining marketing efforts all contribute to sustaining business growth. Attending industry events, engaging with professional networks, and leveraging social media platforms can help broaden your reach. Partnerships with complementary businesses provide access to new customer bases and additional sales channels.

A well-planned marketing strategy keeps your brand visible. Maintaining a calendar of promotional activities, optimizing digital presence, and regularly engaging customers through social media and email marketing ensures consistent outreach. Recognition through industry awards can further boost credibility, attracting more customers and reinforcing trust.

Strengthening Customer Loyalty

Developing a base of repeat customers reduces reliance on new customer acquisition while increasing revenue stability. Implementing loyalty and referral programs rewards existing customers for their continued support and encourages word-of-mouth marketing. Engaging with customers through personalized offers, exclusive discounts, and targeted email campaigns helps strengthen relationships.

Providing outstanding customer service remains a key differentiator. Promptly addressing concerns, ensuring product consistency, and following up on interactions contribute to long-term satisfaction and brand advocacy.

Continuous Development and Innovation

Expanding product or service offerings is crucial for maintaining relevance in a competitive market. Developing new products begins with thorough market analysis and customer feedback. Testing concepts before full-scale launches allows businesses to refine offerings based on real-world insights. Once validated, strategic product launches—supported by social media campaigns and promotional events—drive initial interest and maximize sales potential.

Sustained business success requires ongoing refinement of strategies, proactive market analysis, and a strong commitment to customer satisfaction. By continuously evaluating performance, nurturing customer relationships, and fostering innovation, businesses can maintain growth and outperform competitors in the long run.

CHAPTER LVII

Overseeing Your Finances

Effective Financial Management for Business Stability

Managing finances efficiently is critical to ensuring your business remains sustainable and profitable. Keeping accurate financial records, tracking cash flow, and making informed decisions based on financial data help businesses stay resilient in a competitive market.

Maintaining Accurate Records

Accurate bookkeeping allows businesses to monitor cash flow, evaluate profits and losses, and make sound financial decisions. Establishing a system for tracking income and expenses, whether manually or through accounting software, ensures transparency and helps in tax preparation. Categorizing financial transactions into fixed and variable costs provides a clear picture of operational expenses.

Fixed costs, such as rent, insurance, and employee salaries, remain stable, whereas variable costs, like raw materials, hourly wages, and utility bills, fluctuate based on business activity. Understanding these costs enables better budgeting and cost-control measures.

Forecasting and Planning

Maintaining up-to-date financial records allows businesses to anticipate revenue and expenses, particularly in industries with seasonal fluctuations. Accurate financial forecasting is essential for securing loans or attracting investors. Keeping receipts and tracking both cash and electronic payments prevent discrepancies and streamline tax filing.

Understanding business costs is fundamental to profitability. Fixed costs provide predictability, whereas variable costs offer flexibility. By analyzing these expenses, businesses can optimize financial planning and implement cost-cutting strategies when needed.

Managing Budgets and Cash Flow

Effective cash flow management ensures that a business can meet its financial obligations while maintaining operations. Setting up a system to track cash flow from the outset helps manage expenses efficiently. Regularly comparing actual cash flow with projected figures allows businesses to identify discrepancies and make adjustments.

A contingency fund is crucial for handling unexpected expenses. Delayed payments from customers can negatively impact cash flow, so implementing a structured invoicing system and offering early payment incentives help mitigate risks. Selling slow-moving inventory at a discount can free up cash, while promotional campaigns can increase sales and revenue.

Ensuring Financial Sustainability

To maintain a positive cash flow, businesses should consider spreading costs, negotiating supplier terms, and using company credit cards strategically. Managing inventory efficiently prevents overstocking and ensures that capital isn't tied up unnecessarily.

While some large corporations operate at a loss in their early years, relying on investor funding, most startups need to balance profitability with growth. Understanding financial concepts such as burn rate, liquidity, and net worth helps businesses make informed financial decisions.

By continuously monitoring financial health, maintaining organized records, and strategically managing cash flow, businesses can ensure long-term stability and success.

CHAPTER LVIII

Running the Business

Building and Managing a Strong Business Team

Running a business requires wearing multiple hats, especially in the early stages. However, as the business expands, managing every aspect alone becomes impractical. At some point, delegating responsibilities and assembling a strong team is necessary for sustained growth and efficiency.

Recognizing the Need for Delegation

Initially, many entrepreneurs handle everything themselves to cut costs. While this approach can work in the short term, it may limit the business's ability to scale. Evaluating personal strengths and weaknesses is key—acknowledging when tasks become overwhelming allows for timely delegation. The first step is to hire one or two managers who can oversee major operational areas. As the business continues to grow, additional team members can be introduced, creating a well-structured organization.

Establishing Key Management Areas

Dividing business functions into specialized roles ensures smooth operations. The core areas of management include:

- Production/Operations: Oversees product development, supply chains, and manufacturing to maintain quality and efficiency.
- Human Resources (HR): Manages recruitment, training, employee relations, and workplace culture.
- Sales/Marketing: Focuses on customer acquisition, branding, and promotional strategies to drive revenue.
- Finance: Handles budgeting, cash flow management, and financial planning to ensure stability.
- Customer Service: Maintains customer satisfaction, resolves complaints, and fosters long-term relationships.

Choosing an Effective Organizational Structure

As the team grows, selecting the right structure is crucial for maintaining order and accountability. Some common business structures include:

- Function-Based Structure: A traditional setup where departments (marketing, sales, production, etc.) operate independently with specialized roles. This structure is effective for stable, established businesses.
- Team-Based Structure: A more collaborative and flexible approach, where cross-functional teams work together on projects. While it promotes adaptability, it requires strong coordination to prevent inefficiencies.
- Network Structure: Common in technology-driven and creative industries, this decentralized model allows teams to work autonomously while still aligning with broader company goals.

Regardless of the structure chosen, it must be adaptable to changing business needs.

The Role of IT in Business Growth

In today's digital landscape, IT plays a critical role in maintaining communication, data security, and operational efficiency. Whether through automation, cloud computing, or cybersecurity measures, investing in IT infrastructure is necessary to support the business's digital needs.

Scaling Management Over Time

As the business expands, the management structure should evolve to keep up with increased complexity. Initially, a simple hierarchy may suffice, with the business owner at the top and a few managers overseeing operations. Over time, additional leadership layers can be introduced to provide better oversight and accountability.

Dividing Responsibilities for Efficiency

A well-organized management team divides functions efficiently, enabling each department to focus on its core tasks. Assigning responsibilities to managers allows the business owner to focus on strategic planning, innovation, and long-term growth.

By strategically building a team, delegating tasks, and refining the management structure, businesses can optimize operations, foster innovation, and position themselves for sustained success.

CHAPTER LIX

Leading a Team

Leading and Managing a Growing Team

As your business expands, shifting from handling everything yourself to leading a team becomes a necessity. Effective leadership involves setting clear goals, creating a sense of shared purpose, and ensuring that everyone is aligned toward common objectives. One of the most effective ways to achieve this is by implementing the SMART goal-setting approach.

SMART Goal-Setting for Business Success

Setting clear, measurable goals ensures your team understands what is expected and stays motivated. The SMART method provides a structured way to establish goals:

- Specific – Goals should be precise and clearly defined. Instead of saying "increase sales," set a specific target like "increase sales by 20% in the next three months." This clarity helps your team stay focused.
- Measurable – Goals must be trackable, allowing progress to be assessed. This could be done by monitoring sales numbers, website traffic, or customer inquiries.
- Achievable – Goals should be realistic based on available resources, ensuring they are neither too easy nor impossible. If extra staff or tools are needed, consider

what adjustments must be made.

- Realistic – A goal should be attainable within current business constraints. If your team is at full capacity, doubling output without increasing resources may be unrealistic.
- Time-Based – Setting a deadline for achieving the goal ensures accountability. A timeline like "launch a new product by the end of the quarter" keeps tasks on schedule and allows for better planning.

Using the SMART framework aligns your team toward well-defined objectives, increasing efficiency and the likelihood of achieving business success.

Building a High-Performing Team

Your employees are a crucial part of your business's success. Investing in their growth and well-being leads to increased engagement, productivity, and loyalty.

- Set Clear Goals and Rewards – Motivating employees with clear expectations and performance-based incentives encourages them to take ownership of their work.
- Cultivate a Positive Work Culture – A supportive work environment, built on shared values and trust, enhances collaboration and morale.
- Lead by Example – Your behavior sets the standard. Being punctual, professional, and positive influences your team's attitude and work ethic.
- Communicate Consistently – Transparency in company goals, challenges, and expectations builds trust and ensures employees feel informed. Regular meetings help

align efforts and encourage feedback.

- Turn Mistakes into Learning Opportunities – Instead of penalizing mistakes, encourage employees to learn from them. A growth mindset fosters innovation and continuous improvement.

Encouraging Flexibility in a Growing Business

As your business evolves, ensuring productivity while keeping staff costs manageable is a balancing act. Flexibility in roles and work hours can help maximize efficiency and keep employees engaged.

- Consult Employees Before Implementing Changes – Before adjusting roles or schedules, discuss potential changes with employees to gain their input and ensure a smooth transition.
- Offer Flexibility in Return – If employees are expected to be adaptable with their tasks or schedules, provide them with the option to adjust their hours when needed.
- Listen to Employee Feedback – Employees working on the front lines often have valuable insights into improving processes. Encouraging open discussions can lead to better efficiency and job satisfaction.

Creating an adaptable work environment where employees feel valued and heard contributes to a more motivated and engaged team. By implementing structured goal-setting, fostering a strong workplace culture, and promoting flexibility, you lay the foundation for long-term business success.

CHAPTER LX

Business Operations

Optimizing Business Operations for Efficiency and Growth

Understanding and refining your business operations is essential for maximizing efficiency, reducing costs, and ensuring smooth service delivery. By mapping your business processes and optimizing your supply chain, you can streamline operations and improve overall performance.

Mapping Your Business Processes

Visualizing business operations through process mapping helps identify inefficiencies and areas for improvement. By breaking down and sequencing each step in your processes, you can eliminate unnecessary tasks, reduce delays, and ensure that resources are used effectively.

A process map categorizes activities into two types:

- Value-adding activities – Tasks that directly contribute to producing goods or delivering services.
- Non-value-adding activities – Tasks that do not contribute to the end product or service and should be minimized or eliminated.

Regularly reviewing process maps allows businesses to adapt to technological advancements that can simplify workflows and reduce costs. By clearly outlining each step, process maps also help new employees understand business operations quickly and assist in explaining business functions to investors and stakeholders.

Managing and Strengthening Your Supply Chain

A well-organized supply chain is essential for ensuring seamless operations. It involves all the people, processes, and logistics required to deliver products or services to customers. An efficient supply chain reduces waste, minimizes disruptions, and enhances profitability.

Key Steps to Overseeing Your Supply Chain:

1. Understand Every Link in Your Supply Chain

   - Research your suppliers to ensure they align with your business values.
   - Identify the sources of your raw materials or products and evaluate their reliability.

2. Identify Potential Weaknesses

   - Assess risks such as delays, quality issues, and supplier reliability.
   - Monitor supply chain efficiency to prevent bottlenecks.

3. Develop Contingency Plans

    ◦ Prepare for potential disruptions by establishing backup suppliers.
    ◦ Have alternative transportation or distribution strategies ready.

4. Streamline Supply Chain Processes

    ◦ Implement automation and tracking software to enhance efficiency.
    ◦ Reduce reliance on multiple suppliers by consolidating sourcing when possible.

5. Seek Professional Advice and Supplier Insights

    ◦ Collaborate with suppliers to explore ways to optimize processes.
    ◦ Stay updated on industry best practices and emerging supply chain trends.

6. Regularly Review and Adapt

    ◦ Periodically assess supply chain effectiveness.
    ◦ Adjust strategies based on business growth, market shifts, and operational needs.

Understanding the Role of Supply Chains

Every business, regardless of industry, has a supply chain that must function smoothly to avoid inefficiencies and additional costs. For example, an ice-cream shop may have a simple supply chain focused on ingredient sourcing and product storage, whereas a bakery's supply chain might involve ingredient procurement, baking, packaging, and distribution.

Breakdowns in supply chains can lead to:

- Delays in production or delivery.
- Increased costs due to last-minute adjustments.
- Customer dissatisfaction and potential loss of business.

By identifying vulnerabilities—such as dependence on a single supplier for key materials—you can implement strategies to maintain uninterrupted service. Exploring multiple sourcing options or adjusting production models can help ensure product availability even if one link in the supply chain is disrupted.

Proactive Strategies for Supply Chain Resilience

To strengthen operations, businesses should consider a mix of approaches, including:

- Diversifying suppliers to reduce dependence on a single source.
- Building inventory reserves to cushion against supply delays.
- Exploring local suppliers to reduce reliance on international shipping.
- Investing in technology to track and forecast supply needs efficiently.

By consistently evaluating and optimizing business processes and supply chains, you can improve efficiency, reduce costs, and ensure long-term operational success.

CHAPTER LXI

Enhancing Business

Enhancing Business Operations: Balancing Cost, Quality, Speed, and Flexibility

Success in business requires a careful balance between cost efficiency, quality assurance, speed of delivery, and operational flexibility. These four elements interact, and focusing on one at the expense of the others can lead to inefficiencies or customer dissatisfaction. By optimizing each area strategically, you can build a resilient and competitive business.

Prioritizing Quality for Sustainable Growth

Quality is the foundation of any successful business. A commitment to consistently delivering high-quality products or services builds customer trust and brand reputation. Failing to meet quality standards not only damages credibility but also leads to costly rework and refunds. Consistency in quality ensures that customers return, leading to sustainable long-term success. Businesses should implement quality control measures, employee training, and feedback loops to maintain high standards.

Achieving Speed Without Compromising Excellence

Efficiency in business operations directly impacts costs and customer satisfaction. Faster production or service delivery can reduce expenses and increase competitiveness, but it must be managed carefully to avoid sacrificing quality. Leveraging technology, automation, and streamlined workflows can help accelerate processes without reducing service standards. A balance between speed and precision ensures reliability while meeting market demands effectively.

Building Flexibility for Market Adaptability

Flexibility enables businesses to adjust quickly to customer needs, market trends, and unexpected challenges. Being able to modify product offerings, service delivery, or supply chain operations ensures resilience in a competitive environment. Businesses should establish adaptable processes that allow for customization, urgent orders, or quick pivots when necessary. While maintaining a core operational structure, having room for flexibility prevents stagnation and keeps the business relevant.

Managing Costs Without Undermining Business Performance

Cost optimization should come after ensuring quality, speed, and flexibility are in place. Cutting costs too early can lead to lower customer satisfaction and reduced efficiency. Instead of focusing on cost-cutting alone, businesses should aim for strategic cost management—finding ways to enhance productivity and efficiency while maintaining value. Investing in process improvements, energy efficiency, and supplier negotiations can lead to long-term financial sustainability.

Optimizing Business Processes for Continuous Improvement

Small businesses often struggle with operational inefficiencies that hinder growth. Regularly assessing business performance and making adjustments can improve efficiency, reduce costs, and enhance customer satisfaction.

Incremental vs. Rapid Business Improvements

- Gradual Enhancements involve making small, continuous improvements in processes, workflows, and customer service. This method allows businesses to refine operations without overwhelming their teams.
- Step-Change Adjustments involve making significant operational shifts, such as eliminating underperforming products, outsourcing certain functions, or adopting new technology. While riskier, these changes can drive rapid growth.

Encouraging employees to actively participate in process improvements fosters innovation and efficiency. Creating a culture of continuous improvement helps businesses stay competitive and adaptable.

Documenting Operations for Consistency and Growth

As businesses expand, developing an operations manual becomes essential. A well-documented guide outlines processes, employee roles, standard operating procedures, and emergency protocols. This not only improves efficiency and consistency but also makes onboarding new employees easier. Additionally, having a structured operations manual increases the business's attractiveness to potential investors or buyers, as it demonstrates scalability and structured management.

Crisis Preparedness and Business Continuity

No business is immune to unexpected challenges. Preparing for potential crises—such as supply chain disruptions, data breaches, or financial downturns—ensures stability and continuity.

Developing a Crisis Response Plan

1. Identify Potential Risks – Assess both internal (staffing, product failures) and external (natural disasters, economic downturns) threats to business operations.
2. Plan for Contingencies – Establish action plans for each risk scenario, including alternative suppliers, emergency funds, and remote work capabilities.
3. Establish Clear Communication – Ensure employees, suppliers, and customers receive timely and transparent information during crises.
4. Conduct Crisis Drills – Regularly test business continuity plans through mock scenarios to identify weaknesses and areas for improvement.

Being prepared for disruptions minimizes downtime and allows businesses to adapt quickly, reducing losses and maintaining customer trust.

Maximizing Operational Resilience in the Supply Chain

A well-managed supply chain ensures the smooth flow of products or services. Businesses that actively monitor and refine their supply chain can reduce costs, prevent delays, and improve efficiency.

Key Supply Chain Optimization Strategies

- Assess Supplier Reliability – Work with suppliers that align with business values and maintain quality standards.
- Develop Backup Solutions – Have contingency suppliers or alternative sourcing options in case of disruptions.
- Streamline Logistics – Use technology to track inventory, reduce waste, and optimize delivery routes.
- Strengthen Collaboration – Build strong relationships with suppliers and partners to improve coordination and problem-solving.

Regular reviews of supply chain operations ensure that businesses can respond to market changes and challenges effectively.

Achieving Business Efficiency Through the Sand Cone Model

The Sand Cone Model provides a structured approach to improving business operations without compromising key performance areas. The model suggests that focusing on quality first lays the foundation for further improvements in speed, flexibility, and cost management. Businesses that rush to cut costs before optimizing other factors risk inefficiencies and reduced competitiveness.

1. Quality – Establish a strong foundation by ensuring product and service consistency.
2. Speed – Improve efficiency in processes while maintaining high standards.
3. Flexibility – Build adaptability to handle varying customer needs.
4. Cost – Reduce costs strategically without affecting quality or service reliability.

By prioritizing these steps, businesses can maintain operational excellence while optimizing costs in a sustainable way.

Ensuring Long-Term Business Success

Running a business successfully requires a balanced approach to cost efficiency, quality assurance, operational speed, and flexibility. By systematically improving business processes, monitoring supply chains, preparing for potential crises, and following structured improvement models, businesses can sustain long-term success.

Regular assessment of business performance and proactive planning ensures that small businesses remain resilient, adaptable, and competitive in an ever-changing market.

CHAPTER LXII

Utilizing Technology

Harnessing Technology for Business Growth

In today's competitive landscape, technology plays a vital role in increasing efficiency, improving communication, and enhancing customer engagement. Implementing the right digital tools can streamline operations and help businesses scale effectively. Here's how you can integrate technology strategically to drive growth.

Enhancing Productivity with Technology

Technology offers several ways to optimize business processes and improve workplace efficiency.

Portable Hardware for Flexibility

Laptops, tablets, and external drives allow employees to work remotely, increasing productivity by enabling seamless access to files from anywhere. Businesses can also integrate cloud storage solutions, ensuring that data is not only portable but also secure and easily accessible.

Utilizing Free and Cost-Effective Software

Startups and small businesses can benefit from free and open-source software for accounting, project management, communication, and design. While choosing software, it's crucial to ensure compatibility with existing systems and prioritize security to protect sensitive business data.

Digital Communication for Seamless Collaboration

Tools like Zoom, Microsoft Teams, and Google Meet enable global communication, making it easier to connect with employees, suppliers, and customers. Real-time collaboration tools such as Slack and Trello enhance project management, ensuring teams remain aligned and productive.

Improving Customer Engagement with Technology

Engaging with customers digitally can lead to higher satisfaction, increased sales, and stronger brand loyalty.

Online Support Systems for Better Customer Service

Implementing live chat tools, AI-driven chatbots, and helpdesk apps helps businesses provide instant responses to customer inquiries. Offering 24/7 customer support through automated systems builds trust and increases customer retention.

Leveraging Digital Marketing for Greater Reach

Social media marketing, email campaigns, and search engine optimization (SEO) allow businesses to connect with their target audience at a lower cost compared to traditional advertising. Paid ads on platforms like Google Ads and Facebook provide highly targeted exposure, leading to a better return on investment (ROI).

Data-Driven Insights for Personalization

Analyzing customer data helps businesses tailor marketing efforts, personalize recommendations, and improve service delivery. CRM (Customer Relationship Management) software, such as Salesforce or HubSpot, allows businesses to track customer interactions and anticipate needs.

Optimizing Operations Through Technology

Efficiency is key to business growth. Using technology in day-to-day operations can streamline processes and reduce costs.

Cloud Computing for Scalability

Cloud-based platforms eliminate the need for expensive IT infrastructure while providing secure and scalable storage solutions. Services like Google Drive, Dropbox, and AWS allow businesses to store, share, and back up critical data easily.

Mobile Technology for Convenience

With the increasing reliance on mobile devices, businesses can leverage mobile apps and NFC (Near-Field Communication) technology to facilitate transactions, improve customer experience, and stay connected with their audience. Mobile-friendly websites and payment solutions like Google Pay and Apple Pay further enhance convenience.

Automating Business Processes

Automation tools can reduce manual effort and improve accuracy in various functions such as:

- Accounting & Finance: Software like QuickBooks and Xero automates invoicing, expense tracking, and payroll management.
- Inventory Management: AI-powered inventory systems monitor stock levels in real time, reducing overstock and shortages.
- Marketing Automation: Email marketing tools like Mailchimp and ConvertKit automate personalized campaigns, saving time while increasing engagement.

Ensuring Data Security in a Digital Age

As businesses grow, they accumulate large volumes of customer and operational data. Protecting this data is critical to preventing cyber threats and maintaining trust.

Implementing Cybersecurity Measures

Basic security protocols like firewalls, encrypted cloud storage, and multi-factor authentication (MFA) should be implemented to prevent unauthorized access. Businesses should also invest in cybersecurity training to educate employees on phishing scams and data protection.

Regular Data Backups

Automated backups ensure that essential business data is not lost due to system failures or cyberattacks. Cloud-based backup solutions provide additional security by storing copies in offsite locations.

Compliance with Data Protection Regulations

Understanding and following data privacy laws ensures that businesses handle customer information responsibly. Adhering to these regulations protects against legal issues and enhances brand credibility.

Leveraging Technology for Smarter Growth

Embracing technology is no longer optional—it's a necessity for businesses looking to scale efficiently. Whether through cloud computing, digital marketing, automation, or cybersecurity, technology provides the tools to enhance operations and customer experience. By strategically integrating digital solutions, businesses can streamline processes, drive sales, and build a foundation for long-term success.

CHAPTER LXIII

Scaling Your Business

Scaling Your Business for Sustainable Growth

Expanding a business requires strategic planning, strong leadership, and financial readiness. As your operations grow, ensuring efficiency, customer retention, and team alignment will be critical for sustained success. Here's how to effectively manage and promote business growth while maintaining stability.

Managing Growth Effectively

Hiring and Retaining Skilled Employees

As your business scales, hiring the right talent is crucial. Focus on recruiting adaptable employees who bring innovation and expertise. Invest in leadership training to ensure your team can handle increasing responsibilities. Employee satisfaction directly impacts productivity, so create a strong company culture that values growth and learning.

Optimizing Cash Flow

Growth requires financial resources, and maintaining a positive cash flow is essential. Efficient invoicing, reducing overhead costs, and securing access to credit can help ensure that expansion efforts don't strain your finances. Consider alternative funding sources such as business loans, investors, or government grants to support scaling.

Implementing Scalable Systems

Technology plays a key role in managing increased demand. Automate operations with CRM systems, accounting software, and inventory management tools to improve efficiency. Cloud-based solutions allow seamless collaboration and reduce manual work, ensuring smooth growth without operational bottlenecks.

Expanding Customer Reach

Building Strong Customer Relationships

Retaining existing customers is as crucial as acquiring new ones. Provide exceptional service, loyalty programs, and personalized experiences to keep customers engaged. Happy customers not only return but also recommend your business to others, driving organic growth.

Reaching New Customers

Expanding your audience requires a combination of digital marketing, strategic partnerships, and targeted outreach. Utilize SEO, social media marketing, influencer collaborations, and referral programs to attract new customers and increase brand awareness.

Consistent Marketing Investment

Scaling businesses must maintain consistent marketing efforts. Running paid advertising campaigns, engaging in content marketing, and hosting events help build credibility and attract new leads. Adjust strategies based on customer behavior and performance data to maximize impact.

Strategies for Expansion

Introducing New Products or Services

Diversifying your offerings can increase revenue streams and attract different customer segments. Consider complementary products that align with your current line or develop entirely new services to meet evolving market demands.

Business Acquisitions

Acquiring a business that aligns with your industry can accelerate expansion. Merging with a related company gives you access to an existing customer base, infrastructure, and talent, often making it more cost-effective than building from scratch.

Forming Strategic Partnerships

Collaborating with other businesses can reduce costs and create mutual benefits. Partnerships in marketing, distribution, or product development allow shared resources and expertise, making it easier to enter new markets.

Regional and Global Expansion

Expanding to new geographical areas can boost revenue, whether through opening new locations, franchising, or expanding online sales internationally. Before entering a new region, conduct thorough market research to understand local customer preferences and competition.

Choosing the Right Growth Strategy

Every business has unique goals and resources, so selecting the right expansion strategy is crucial:

- Market Penetration – Increase sales within your existing market by attracting more customers, enhancing promotions, or adjusting pricing strategies.

- Market Development – Expand into new geographic regions or demographics to tap into fresh customer segments.
- Product Development – Innovate and launch new products or improved versions to meet customer needs and stay competitive.
- Diversification – Enter new industries or markets with unique offerings, but approach this strategy cautiously due to the higher risks involved.

Funding Expansion

Securing funding for growth requires preparation and careful planning:

- Improve Financial Records – Maintain clear, up-to-date financial documentation to attract investors or lenders.
- Strengthen Credit Scores – A strong credit score increases the likelihood of securing financing at favorable terms.
- Create a Comprehensive Business Plan – A well-structured plan demonstrates how additional funds will be used effectively.
- Consider Multiple Funding Sources – Explore business loans, venture capital, crowdfunding, or grants as financing options.
- Monitor Cash Flow Implications – Ensure that new investments and loans do not disrupt daily operations.

Scaling with Confidence

Expanding a business is an exciting but challenging process that requires clear objectives, strong leadership, and financial stability. By focusing on customer retention, strategic expansion, and operational efficiency, businesses can scale effectively while maintaining long-term success.

CHAPTER LXIV

Reflections

India's entrepreneurial landscape is a testament to resilience, innovation, and an unwavering spirit of enterprise. Over the years, the nation has cultivated a thriving startup ecosystem, backed by government initiatives, evolving financial support structures, and a culture that encourages risk-taking and creativity. Yet, entrepreneurship is not without its hurdles. Regulatory complexities, intense market competition, and resource constraints challenge even the most determined individuals. However, these very obstacles serve as catalysts for innovation, disruption, and long-lasting impact.

Let's take a moment to reflect on the essential insights we've gathered:

1. Mindset Shapes Success

The foundation of entrepreneurship lies in cultivating the right mindset—one that embraces challenges, persists through setbacks, and views failure as a stepping stone to growth. Passion and perseverance remain the driving forces behind sustainable success.

2. Knowledge Fuels Growth

A well-equipped entrepreneur is one who continuously learns and adapts. From market research to financial literacy, understanding the intricacies of business operations is critical. Lifelong learning and a commitment to self-improvement serve as powerful tools for overcoming obstacles.

3. The Strength of Community

Success is rarely achieved in isolation. Strong networks, mentorship, and collaboration open doors to opportunities, insights, and support systems that can accelerate business growth. In an interconnected world, leveraging relationships is as vital as developing skills.

4. Purpose-Driven Entrepreneurship

True entrepreneurial success goes beyond profit—it is about impact. Businesses that align purpose with profitability not only sustain themselves but also contribute positively to society. Solving real-world challenges, fostering inclusivity, and driving social change elevate entrepreneurship to a meaningful pursuit.

India's entrepreneurial journey continues to inspire, evolve, and expand. Whether you are just starting out or refining an existing venture, remember that entrepreneurship is not just about building businesses—it's about shaping the future. Stay resilient, keep learning, and never lose sight of the purpose behind your vision.